Emerge Victorious

· · ·

A Woman's Transformational Guide After Her Divorce

· · ·

Melissa,

best wishes
Jennifer Cisney

Melissa,
Love & Blessings
Sandra Dopf Lee

By

Sandra Dopf-Lee and Jennifer Cisney

xulon
PRESS

Emerge Victorious
A Woman's Transformational Guide After Her Divorce
by Sandra Dopf Lee and Jennifer Cisney

Printed in the United States of America

ISBN 9781613798072

Unless otherwise indicated, Bible quotations are taken from The American Standard Version.

www.xulonpress.com

Emerge Victorious

● ● ●

A Woman's Transformational Guide After Her Divorce

● ● ●

*E*very gorgeous butterfly, with her wings spread open and her brilliant colors on display, has undergone a great change—a transformation in the comforts of her own private cocoon. Before that butterfly could even think about taking flight, she had to learn to crawl. She had to learn to be ok in her own small space. She had to adapt to the depths of darkness before she could see the light. And then, just when she didn't think she could breathe even one more breath, she broke out of her prison and set herself free.

We feel so honored that you have chosen to hold this book in your hands. We have prayed for you and God has answered those prayers by leading you to this message scribed specifically for you. Are you that caterpillar just learning to crawl? Or are you bound up so tight in your cocoon that you just can't find the air to breathe?

We like to refer to the divorce process in stages, similar to that of a gorgeous butterfly who emerges from the depths of the forgotten world after self-assessment, transformation and hope for what lies ahead. We joke sometimes about how we compartmentalize time: "B.D." (before divorce) and "A.D." (after divorce). Although there is much to learn in the "B.D." of your life story, we are here to help you navigate through the beginning stages of "A.D." and beyond. Just remember, the beauty of a butterfly comes only after hard work and commitment to change. This book is your first step to Emerge Victorious through your great transformation. Let's get started...

Thank You

To all of the women that we've had the privilege of walking with you through and beyond your divorce, you have taught us so much as we've worked together during all the unknowns of your divorce, all the while seeking to be a living testimony of God's healing love and redemptive plan. You are amazing women!

To Gretchen, your encouragement, humor and wisdom are inspiring and you continue to lead us onward. This book, and many of the other Emerge Victorious projects, simply wouldn't exist without you! When God laid His vision on our heart, we didn't know He had an angel waiting to carry us on her wings.

To Nicole, your remarkable way with words has been an amazing gift. The purpose and passion of this book is to help women to not "opt out" of their role in God's story being lived out through them – even when divorce has interrupted their lives. You are a living example of both, exemplified through your own life and your words.

To you – the reader, we pray for you and your journey as you courageously start over after your divorce. We humbly hope there are some messages or transformational exercises in this book that will be valuable in your growth. YOU are the reason for <u>Emerge Victorious</u> – YOU are significant – YOU are valuable – YOU are loved!

Love and Blessings,
Sandra and Jennifer

* * *

Introduction

* * *

*D*ivorce has written messages on your life's canvas and in the chapters of your story thus far. Some of those messages may be continuing to paralyze you through their power, which is robbing you of your hopes and your dreams. As you prepare for a great transformation, are you ready to set up your easel and attach a clean canvas? Take out your paint brush and begin your new life story; one of vision, strength, beauty and all that lies within you.

Just because divorce is now part of your story, the basic issues of life don't go away. There is still loneliness, financial challenges and parenting pressures. As you get a better hold on grappling with anger, joy, grief, endings and beginnings, you prepare yourself to confront a new start. This requires the tools of guidance, hope, energy and encouragement. It's not just about the legal papers that need to be filed, but more about the architecture of your new life, your identity and connections to your future. It is about where you go from "here." You may have felt that you have handed your life over to sheer existence. The questions of your abilities and whether you are too old, or equipped to build a thriving life may be plaguing you. This book is a working guide to taking the next steps to move beyond those doubts. As you emerge, so will other aspects of your life as you begin to transform.

You are facing a profound transition. As with any major life change, the hardest aspects of divorce are the ambiguities and loss of control as you try and define a "new" normal. Comforting routines, cherished activities, and personal securities disappear and you begin the search for new ones. How many of us women structured our lives around "until death do us part?" It takes time to adjust in this desert landscape. Life is never the same after divorce (and sometimes that is a good thing), but rest assured the sun does shine again. You must allow yourself time to grieve and then choose to embrace change and search for a new beginning.

Let's do something different, ladies, together – one step, one chapter at a time. There is no way around it – divorce hurts, divorce is scary, divorce is lonely, divorce changes lives, but your reality is: divorce has interrupted your life. It is a significant process to go through, but it does not have to define you and it does not have the power to deny you the rest of your life. Yes, the enormity of change ushered in along with the emotional, financial, and relational challenges, and the welcomed or un-welcomed compliments of divorce are daunting. Only you have the authority to allow divorce to rob you of how you live your life. We know from personal experience, and walking alongside many others, that transforming your life from survival and existence into a thriving life following a divorce is not only possible, but attainable. Just hoping for change and a fresh start isn't enough. You need tools for creating a vision and you need to implement a plan of action to move forward. We believe in your power to be successful on your journey as you reinvent yourself. There are two roads before you, and we hope you choose the one that winds toward a thriving life and you are no longer willing to settle for a mere survival.

The time is now to shift your thinking. Your growth is the pasion behind the writing of ***Emerge Victorious: A Woman's Transformational Guide After Her Divorce***. You are embarking on a transformational process to work through the effects of your divorce and set yourself free to live the life God has waiting for you.

Two hearts, two minds, came together to co-author this book. As God would design it, the two of us met in 2006 while attending a conference in Memphis, Tennessee. Sandra sitting on her bed in pajamas, her hair pulled up in a ponytail and wearing no make-up, and Jennifer dressed in black pants and a jean jacket, hair perfect and beautiful. Just like that—God brought us together as part of His big plan and within moments, two strangers were sharing divorce stories and a common thread for guiding, equipping and encouraging divorced women to rise up and live an abundant and intentional life. This book was birthed out of personal experiences with our own divorces, combined with over 25 cumulative years of working with divorced clients from all over the nation. We also share a passion for training others to work in the mission field of divorce. Please don't disqualify this message due to our being fallible messengers. We do not begin to boast that we can offer you all the answers and give your life back all tidied up, wrapped nicely in pretty paper with a big bow on top. What we can offer is this practical, honest, and passionate book along with growth exercises that we believe can be life changing in guiding you out of the "stuck" places of your divorce and into the life that is waiting on you! But we need YOU to actively pursue your honest truth and do the work that lies ahead of you. God doesn't take away our battles, but He does offer us strength, wisdom and other people and resources to help stand in the gap.

Too tired to hear the words "work"? We get that. But aren't you tired of living the way you are right now? Isn't that why you have picked up this book in the first place? With each step you achieve, view it as the next step into a much bigger venture – yes, the end of one journey – but the beginning of another.

In his book, Pursuit of Holiness, Jerry Bridges explains of how people cannot throw out the seeds for a harvest crop and then just return to the porch and pray for the crops to grow. He shares how we (people) must do the work of preparing the soil, planting the seeds, watering the crops, pulling the weeds; and yes, also praying and trusting the Lord with the outcome. This is the time to plant a new crop in your life, work the process, pray, live and grow!

In 1968, John Stephen Akhwari, a marathon runner from Tanzania, competed in the Mexico City Olympics. At the start of the race he fell and was badly injured. Four and a half hours later, a wincing Akhwari, bloodied and bandaged, limped into the stadium and crossed the finish line. When a reporter interviewed him following the race, he asked, "Why did you not retire?" Akhwari replied, "My country didn't send me to start the race, they sent me to finish it." God has sent us to run a race this side of heaven and therefore, quitting should not be an option. We need to keep our eyes focused on eternity. When we cross the finish line, we will hear His words of how well we ran, even in the midst of our trials and circumstances.

Now, we need to have a little discussion about how this book has been written. First, we (Jennifer and Sandra) would prefer sitting in the living room, over something warm to drink and tasty to eat while working through these chapters with you week after week (and who knows, maybe one day we will get to meet you). Since we can't sit all cozy on the couch, the next best option was putting this book together and offering so much love, passion and encouragement for all the women who read it. Although we cannot physically be there with you on the other side of these pages, we pray you will grow beyond your divorce. As co-authors, we have added a personal message from each of us regarding the topic of discussion. We believe this allows more of you to identify with our own unique divorce life experiences and our individual stories of working with other divorced women. We have walked a mile in those shoes you are wearing, and so have many, many others before you. You are not alone.

Our book has been written to be read, worked and lived out. We do not think of it as a "great piece of reading mateial" but rather an authentic companion as you step forward in regaining your life.

We have a directive approach and style, for there isn't time to waste! Your life and future are too important for softness and coddling. We ask you to be honest with your reality. You cannot change what you are not willing to acknowledge and confront. Change begins with the decision to be real, truthful and ready to invest in the steps it takes to get you from the parts of your life you aren't happy with to the life you wish to live.

We offer "transformation exercises" in each chapter which have been specifically designed for your own individual growth through reflection and self-discovery. To get as much as you can from this book, we strongly urge you to complete these important assignments. Take your pen out. Write in your book, use a spiral notebook or if you bought our journal – use whatever works best for you. Spend some time with the questions. Don't rush. Find some place to be alone with you and your book – this time is for you. Putting you first, being the best you, will enable you to offer back to the Lord, to your children, to your extended family, to your friends, to your job, and when, or if, the time comes to another special person.

We all participate in life but **how** we participate is up to us as individuals. We will serve as your personal coaches throughout these pages. Let's begin designing the kind of participation that leads you to a life you will be proud to leave as your legacy. Are you ready to live a conscious life? One that mirrors your values, is filled with hope, and creates memories? A life designed by you for you? If you are saying, "Yes, I am ready", then grab a cup of coffee or tea and let's spend some quality time together through words, scripture, guidance and actions taken by you. As we journey together, it is our prayer that your life vision awakens with purpose and a plan.

Let's start with some introductions:

Hi, I am Sandra.

Today, my life is renewed, and I am passionate and purposeful about how I am living my life and excited to see what God has in store for the rest of my days; but let me tell you, there was a time when I was an absolute mess and afraid of the unknowns I was facing because of divorce. Divorce wasn't a path I ever wanted to choose for myself or my children, but it is a path I have walked down not once, but twice.

As for what makes up this season in my life today, I spend time reading, riding my bike, with a cute little basket attached, around Daniel Island in Charleston, South Carolina, boating, and traveling to see the beautiful landscape of the United States. I do enjoy spending time with my three children. My sons, Blake and Ryan, are in their mid-twenties, and my daughter, Kristen, is headed off to college. They simply don't have much time to spend with their mom at this time in their lives, so, I enjoy occasional dinners, a movie or a blessed weekend/holiday when I get some "chunks" of time with them.

So how did two divorces happen? Remarriage too quickly after my first divorce (I thought my ex was my only problem and I was ready to be married again – wrong!). See, honestly, my divorce began when I was five years old. My father was killed and my mother found her coping skills through alcohol and prescription drugs. Hello abandonment, fears and insecurity (to name a few). I also learned a few coping skills of my own from my childhood that rendered a woman using control, perfection and many false masks in relating to my husband and to my life as a whole. My wish isn't to share the ways and faults of my ex-husbands, but to focus on my story. I am not saying neither of my ex-husbands had any responsibility for the demise of our marriages, or even my childhood, but I am choosing to share about the common denominator here – me (there are so many details and maybe one day that will be another book when and if the time comes). What I can say loudly is blended family life, unresolved relationship issues and lack of individual healthiness is not a recipe for a healthy marriage or remarriage.

Nine years after committing to a second marriage, I found myself saying good-bye to another one. With feelings of shame, guilt (especially for my children) and two failed marriages in tow, I faced those fears I had already battled both as a child and at the end of my first marriage. How would I support three kids as a single mother? How would God possibly forgive me for two divorces? How would people view me and my kids (as damaged goods)? How would I ever live a life of any hope or value? I was filled with anger at myself for "doing it again" and full of questions for God for all those unanswered prayers. Completely lacking was my vision for a future.

I was tired of the insanity of my life. I didn't want to go through another divorce — I felt so much shame. I wanted to finally move beyond my childhood and my marriages. It could no longer be about the role others had or were playing in my life, not about what others were thinking about me. It had to be a time about me and how I was going to do life differently. It was time to make the choice to be honest with myself about my reality and seek the wisdom and professional help in the areas that needed addressing. So, cradled on the floor, next to the sofa, I released with a vengeance years of bottled up pain with bellowing screams, tears, snot and all. My breaking point had come.

That day was beyond painful. In fact, at times, I wondered if pain and fear would have the power to actually kill me. But that day also held another power – the door to change. On that day, I decided to somehow and some way write the next chapter of life differently; authored with responsibility, healing, letting go, facing my fears and creating a life I wanted to be both participating in and living. It would take time and lots of hard work, but I made a new vow to God to spend the rest of my days to living well.

That woman in the fetal position on the living room floor doesn't resemble the woman sitting here with my laptop writing this book. The journey wasn't paved with ease just because I made a heart-felt decision. However, the intentional choices strung together and growing toward my goal have played a huge part in the person I emerged into over the last 12 years.

I wake each day, my friend, hoping that my life will be a living testimony to how God is waiting to give us the transforming power that He offers to us. Like you, divorce is a part of my story, but it is a chapter (ok, it is several chapters). God has a plan for each of us; we must be willing to join Him. Finally, I removed the masks of perfection, control and over spiritualization to cover my insecurities, to be the real Sandra; broken, sinner, but forgiven child of God. He still loves me and is proud to be my Papa. I hope you, too, will find this resting place in your journey and that this book will be an inspirational tool to help you along the way.

Blessings to you for your journey,
Sandra

Hi, I am Jennifer.
Divorce is a difficult and painful circumstance that I would not wish for anyone. But I can honestly say that God has used my divorce for great change and growth in my life. What I once saw as one of the most tragic events in my life has become an experience that I would not trade. Without the catalyst of my marriage falling

apart, I would likely not have focused energy and time on my own personal growth. I spent over five years in counseling with two different therapists. I faced painful issues from my past and made a commitment to growth and becoming a more honest and authentic person. It is true that God does work all things together for good for those who love Him (Romans 8:28). He was faithful and gracious to use my mistakes, my brokenness and yes - even my divorce - to teach me what He wanted me to know. It was not a quick or easy process. I had to work very hard. But today, I have a life that is better than ever before. I feel better about who I am and where I am going. That is not to say that I don't still make mistakes or face challenges. I certainly do. But I made decisions and a commitment while going through my divorce that still determines how I will face life, pain and disappointment. Without the pain of my divorce, I would not have been equipped to face the challenges I have experienced in the last 15 years. In fact, I am just finishing up another painful and difficult journey as I write this book. I have walked the painful journey of watching my mother face Alzheimer's disease. Almost five years ago, I left my life, my home and my community in Charlotte, NC to move back to my home state of Kentucky to help care for my mother as she battled Alzheimer's. My mother died a few weeks ago. Without the growth I experienced following my divorce, I would never have had the strength or courage to walk this road with my mother. I learned to face into my pain and look for messages in the suffering.

The key decision I made during my divorce was to keep my heart open. It sounds simple, but when I faced disappointment in my marriage and betrayal by someone I loved, my initial response was to close my heart. This is true for many people who face pain, loss or disappointment. Consciously or unconsciously, we feel the best way to keep from being hurt or disappointed again is to stop caring so much. We close our hearts. We care less and feel less. The problem with this choice is that our hearts have only two positions - open and closed. When we close our hearts to love and potential pain, we are also closing our hearts to God, to joy, to life. The quote from C.S. Lewis in his book, <u>The Four Loves</u>, states this dilemma clearly and concisely:

"There is no safe investment. To love at all is to be vulnerable. Love anything, and your heart will certainly be wrung and possibly broken. If you want to make sure of keeping it intact, you must give your heart to no one, not even to an animal. Wrap it carefully round with hobbies and little luxuries; avoid all entanglements; lock it up safe in the casket or coffin of your selfishness. But in that casket - safe, dark, motionless, airless - it will change. It will not be broken; it will become unbreakable, impenetrable, irredeemable. This alternative to tragedy, or at least to the risk of tragedy, is damnation. The only place outside of Heaven where you can be perfectly safe from all the dangers and perturbations of love is Hell."

During the time my marriage was falling apart, God asked me to open my heart. You see, my heart had been closed for many years. This was part of the reason my marriage was dying. God made it clear that I could not love Him or be the person He wanted me to be if I continued through life protecting myself from pain and loss. I had to take a risk. I had to dream again, feel again, and love again. I agreed. I must admit, the consequences of that commitment have been great joy and great sadness. I have experienced grief and loss as well as fulfillment and joy. I learned to dream again. I have experienced disappointments. But I can still say, without hesitation, that it was the right choice.

My wish for you is that in the aftermath of your divorce, you will keep your dreams alive and your heart open.

Blessings,
Jennifer

Ecclesiastes 3: 1-8

*   *   *

For everything there is a season,
and a time for every matter under heaven:
A time to be born, and a time to die;
a time to plant, and a time to pluck up what is planted;
A time to kill, and a time to heal;
a time to break down, and a time to build up;
A time to weep, and a time to laugh;
a time to mourn, and a time to dance;
A time to throw away stones, and a time to gather stones together;
a time to embrace, and a time to refrain from embracing;
A time to seek, and a time to lose;
a time to keep, and a time to throw away;
A time to tear, and a time to sew;
a time to keep silence, and a time to speak;
A time to love, and a time to hate;
a time for war, and a time for peace.

*   *   *

Chapter 1

• • •

Having the Divorce Conversation

• • •

It all began with: "Do you take this man to be your husband?" followed with a very excited, heart-felt "Yes, I do..."

We all share in the fact that we stood facing our ex-spouses and said those words. We all share in the fact that we were pronounced 'husband and wife'. After that, our stories vary and are unique to each of us until we come full circle and all are connected by the word, "divorce". So let's talk about the life in the middle.

Somewhere between "I do" and "I don't" you may have experienced one of the following scenarios:

♦ You dated for years before marriage or you married after a short dating period

♦ You were a Christian before marriage or one of you was a Christian and one wasn't

♦ You sought the divorce or your ex-spouse sought the divorce

♦ You had children, you had no children or you couldn't have children

♦ You have grandchildren

♦ You lost count of how many anniversaries you celebrated or you cherished each one

♦ You had no money conflicts so it was not an issue or money was a key issue

♦ You dealt with infidelity, pornography, abuse, addiction, lying or they did not have a key role

Maybe you can identify with one or all of the above circumstances; maybe you can't identify with one. Only you know the chapters of your life story. Although you might want to, these chapters of your life cannot be rewritten. They are your reality. Looking back, are there any life lessons learned from those experiences? Be prepared to identify those lessons in the 'divorce life assessment' exercise. We promise that you will experience growth from these lessons in the future. You may wish you could have offered a "thank you, but no thanks" and just skipped those life lessons, but you didn't seem to get that option. You have lived the experience, so now what will you do with it?

Divorce has turned your life upside down and inside out and changed your "life-ever-after" direction. Its grip is fierce. You probably jumped on the roller coaster of emotions with bottom-less turns of fear, anger, sadness, tears and questions with few answers that made sense. There are many great resources available to help you as you navigate through the legal process, the emotional process and the financial process that accompanies divorce. (Be sure to reference the resources we provide at the end of this book). However, the purpose of **_Emerge Victorious_** is to help you identify the areas in your "after divorce life" that aren't working well for you and need some changes. God isn't through with you yet, sister, so we need to set the course to live the life you are being called to live.

The Next Conversation

We cannot deny that the word "divorce" conjures up many opinions, views, and countless sermons and books. In fact, it pains us how many Christians tend to wound their own with judgment regarding divorce. We would like to say a few things right here and right now before we go to another page regarding our beliefs and views on the topic:

❖ We (Sandra and Jennifer) are both committed Christians – period. We are sinners
   in need of God's grace and forgiveness. We
   believe we are loved fully by our Father.

❖ We believe God has a purpose and a plan for
   each and every one of us – divorced or not.

❖ We believe in the institution of a healthy
   marriage.

❖ We are not debating anyone's views on
   divorce (biblical or not) in this book.

❖ We are not debating whether divorce is right
   or wrong in this book; nor are we debating
   whether "the divorce" should have taken
   place or not. We are writing to encourage
   and educate women on how to rebuild their
   lives after divorce.

❖ We believe the damage caused in unhealthy
   marriages, the adversarial legal system in
   which dissolution of the marriage occurs,
   and the way people are treated after divorce,
   are devastating and pains us greatly.

❖ We hope women living in God's graces will
   move through and beyond their divorce in
   the healthiest emotional, physical and spiritual steps. We encourage counseling, growth
   groups, reading, prayer, and spending time
   healing and growing before thoughts of
   dating and remarriage.

❖ We believe women who have the right tools of education, support and a vision will foster hope which will allow them to be more open to co-creating a life that will be honoring and pleasing to themselves and God.

❖ We believe the words in Isaiah 53: Jesus bore our grief and carried our sorrow when He left His God power in heaven and became man. He hasn't forsaken us—He knows our pain and fears.

❖ We believe God is a God of forgiveness, offers new beginnings, doesn't abandon us, doesn't label us or devalue us, and certainly hasn't given up on any of His children.

As Christians, it is hard to come to terms with divorce. This is a wrestling match that goes on everyday in the pulpit, in print and in our conversations with other Christians. We hope you find some wisdom and grace-filled counsel to spend time with as you pour through your thoughts and fears regarding your divorce. With that being said, we also hope that you choose to unlock the shackles of shame right now! Shame is not a powerful change agent.

Another Conversation

We know many of you may still be dealing with questions about your divorce as a Christian. Questions such as:

♦ Why did I marry him in the first place?
♦ Did I try hard enough to save my marriage?
♦ Have I ruined my children's lives?
♦ Will God ever forgive me?
♦ Do other Christians perceive me as a woman with the scarlet "D"?
♦ Is happiness off the table for me as a divorced woman?

Having all the answers will take time to process. Seek the answers and healing for the ones you can and choose to let the others go unanswered if they are not doing anything good in creating your future. Don't allow false beliefs to keep you tied to guilt. That simply isn't God's style. Living life from a negative place is detrimental to growth. No one gets married only to begin wondering how life will play out when there is a divorce. In the next chapter of this book, we will look at what you need to do with your divorce process to begin releasing it.

We pray that you feel encouraged, empowered and inspired as you seek to rebuild your life after your divorce with integrity, values and a renewed passion for your future. This will come by beginning to move forward, whether it be a big step or little baby steps; the size doesn't matter. The decision to step is key. For too long now, Christian women have not had the encouragement and guidance on how to start fresh after divorce. There is a fear of the backlash from pastors, churches, and Christians in general, as they sometimes feel that authors, speakers and resources offered on this topic are promoting divorce. We, Jennifer and Sandra, know how much we needed something like the book you are reading and other resources when we went through our own divorces and began the daunting task of rebuilding our life that followed. We also know the need we have encountered over and over as we have worked with other divorced women. Whatever a person's Biblical view on divorce, it hasn't changed that divorce is affecting more than 50% of all women. And, in fact, it is affecting an even higher percentage if we count the children, extended family members and so on. Divorce is affecting lives in your neighborhood, in your church and around the world. We can no longer deny its presence and power in the Christian community and the need to have some good resources to help people rebuild lives after divorce with hope and success.

A Personal Message from Sandra:
When I went through my divorce, I was the director of the Women's Ministry Team at my

church. For years, I kept the pain and dysfunction silent as my family was bleeding to death by little pin holes. It was my pride (my sin) that got in the way of reaching out for help. The mask of being a well-respected Christian family, one that had it all together, whatever that means, was more important to me than the souls of the ones living the lie. Just writing that right now brings tears to my eyes.

I was afraid of failure. I was afraid that I wouldn't be viewed as a "good" Christian and I could no longer wear the hat of director of Women's Ministry. I was afraid the church would tell me what I least wanted to hear: "You are no longer valuable or worthy of being a Christian leader." I was afraid that God's hate for divorce translated into His hate for me, and I couldn't bear that thought. I tried to pretend that the "mess" would all get better – but it didn't. Did I mention I was afraid?

Many of my fears were inaccurate and self-imposed. Fears are often seen through the distorted lenses of our emotional health. Today, I share with you that my emotional well-being wasn't nearly as perfect as the faces I assigned to cover it all up. Some of my fears came to fruition, and I did feel judged at times; but I also *felt loved at times. I had the most wonderful pastor, Mike Moses, and church community. Don and Sally Meredith who came alongside me and walked with me. Here was the couple who founded Christian Family Life; the couple who wrote the book,* <u>Two Becoming One</u>, *over 40 years ago; the couple who was the very pillars of marriage and Christianity; yet it is this couple who embraced me from the moment God placed them in my life—just when I needed them most. Right up to this very moment, I still consider Don and Sally as my mentors and my dearest friends.*

I know from years of walking alongside so many divorced women that they don't share the love and support I received – which is exactly why I am so passionate about the speaking, writing and coaching that I do. I want to offer to them the bridge that was offered to me through relationships.

As a Christian, I also despise divorce and the damage it causes and the lives it affects, but I stand today shouting from my soul to yours, my friend: God DOESN'T hate you, or your family – He may not be pleased with some of your choices and you may suffer from consequences of those choices, but that in no way equates His not loving you! Somewhere in my Christian journey, I got that messed up. I thought if life was hurting, not working well or I was afraid and sad then that translated into being a bad Christian and God not being happy or loving to me. Again, another book and journey, but what I offer here is: that idea is a distorted view I had to work through and I encourage you to do the same.

Sandra

A Personal Message from Jennifer:
I assure you that no little girl dreams of growing up, meeting her handsome prince, getting married and then...after a few years....getting divorced. We all dream of living "happily ever after." We don't imagine that we will become one of the statistics. Regardless of the circumstances of the divorce, it is a difficult and painful process that would not be on a list of situations anyone would choose for their life. But divorce happens. It happens to good, well-intentioned people. Despite our best intentions, we all make mistakes and bad choices. As broken and flawed humans, sometimes our relationships will also become broken. For me, my divorce was a pivotal and life-changing event in my life. While it was a painful situation that I would not have chosen, the end result was that I became a better

person. God stayed true to His word to work all things together for good - even my divorce.

I knew my marriage was in trouble within months of my wedding. Actually, I had doubts and second thoughts before my wedding day. But I kept my denial in place for as long as possible. Within a couple of years, I was beginning to fear I couldn't keep things together. It was clear my husband had an addiction. While I was hiding this from the world, my own internal levels of denial were beginning to collapse. This is when I started to face into the possibility that my marriage might not survive. Having a strong Christian faith, my first concern was how this would impact my relationship with God. What was my responsibility? How did God want me to deal with this situation? I sought counsel from pastors and spiritual leaders (ranging from very helpful to devastating) but I also went to scripture and studying what the Bible really said about divorce. I probably don't have to tell you that there are many different views and interpretations of what scripture says about divorce. My desire is not to tell you what the Bible says, or argue for one point of view over another. In fact, my process of trying to figure this out led me to realize that this is a complicated question and I would not answer these questions for anyone else. But when my husband filed for divorce, it was no longer my choice, but a reality I had to face. I struggled more with the shame of the failure of the marriage than of the actual loss of the relationship. Sad but true. I came to face a few truths about the failure and end of my marriage that have helped me heal and move forward.

First, there is no blameless or innocent party in the failure of a relationship. I had to acknowledge and confess my mistakes, bad choices and selfishness in my marriage and own my role. When I stopped focusing on my husband's faults and mistakes and started focusing on my own, it gave me the power to face my own sins and weaknesses and heal. I cannot change anyone else. However, I can change myself. Knowing what I needed to transform and then taking those steps to get there helped me feel I was taking the measures to assure I would not repeat those mistakes. I owned my role in the failure of my marriage and took steps to change myself and my life in critical ways.

Secondly, grace is powerful enough to cover all our sins, even divorce. Once I had faced my weaknesses and sins, I could embrace a faith *that gave me a chance to start over. Grace is far more powerful than divorce.*

And lastly, your life can be better on the other side of divorce. Satan wanted me to believe that I would never recover from the pain of the divorce and my life would be forever destroyed. The truth is my life today is so much better. This doesn't mean I didn't have painful consequences (emotional, physical, financial) but the internal, spiritual changes that God brought about through the pain of my divorce has made me a more compassionate, authentic and caring person. Before my divorce, I was something of an "elder brother." I was self-righteous and wanted to keep up my facade of having everything together in my life. My divorce was the catalyst to admitting that I was a broken, struggling person in need of a savior. This has enabled me to connect with and love other broken and struggling people in ways I never could have before.

In short, I would never have chosen divorce as a part of my life story. But today, I thank God for using this painful situation to change me in positive ways and draw me closer to Him.

Jennifer

YOUR TRANSFORMATION

Although it is tough to do a self-assessment on ourselves, it is critical to healing and self-discovery. These important transformation exercises are some of those 'first steps' we mentioned:

Divorce-Life Self-Assessment:

1. Identify by writing down the parts of your divorce that you wish you could have handed the "thanks-but-no-thanks" notes to. Which hurts would you have just skipped in your life? If you are wondering why we would have you relive this, it is because we have learned by acknowledging and writing down those thoughts, you have a place to put them so you can release them from your daily life story.

2. Identify the thoughts and beliefs you have as a Christian regarding divorce.

3. Which of those thoughts and beliefs do you still need to work on to be able to move forward?
   ✓ When will you seek counsel (coach, counselor, pastor, and friend)?
   ✓ What book or tape can you read/listen to aid you in your growth? (We have ref-

erenced a few in the back of this book to get you started)
- ✓ Record your "new" thoughts and beliefs next to your "old" belief system when you work through them.

4. How have other Christians been helpful or harmful to you with their attitudes, words, and actions?

5. What do you need to learn from those other Christians and what do you need to let go of?

My Halfway House

• • •

Is in between where I've been and where I'm going
It's almost a home - especially when someone special
Comes to visit halfway between conditions in life
And needs a friend, to listen - a refuge, where sharing is safe,
I feel safe here, although, at times, I do feel lonely.
I've learned many things about myself - living alone.
I'm the same, yet I'm different.
No one can ever replace or be substituted
for that part of me that is gone.
My void is being filled in a new way.
I'm becoming - more totally me -
Halfway between where I've been, and where I'm going.

• • •

By Jan Kruger

Chapter 2

. . .

Saying Goodbye to Your Marriage

. . .

You may be asking yourself: "Didn't I do this already? Didn't I say goodbye on our date of separation? I said goodbye on the day I signed the divorce papers, didn't I? Goodbye was the moment I walked away, wasn't it?" The answer is, "No." Saying "goodbye" goes far deeper than the physical parting of ways. There are emotional and spiritual goodbyes that need to take place and we will help you understand this more clearly in this important chapter.

The landscape of your life has certainly changed. Do you ever wonder if God has "fallen asleep" during this piece of your life? On your wedding day, you thought the ultimate "goodbye" would be death. Well, divorce is a death – just a living death – and certainly not the death you spoke of in your vows, "till death do us part." What happened to that commitment?

There comes a day when you are driving down the road, waking up in the morning, taking your shower, washing the dishes or some daily ritual, and you say to yourself, "I am ready to say goodbye". It has stopped hurting the same way it did. For birth, baptisms, graduations, milestones, birthdays, and death, there are rituals for transitioning from one season of your life to another. Maybe these rituals exist because they come with honor. Society doesn't associate honor with divorce. However, we believe there is power in having a ceremonious goodbye designed for you and by you in order to move forward with your life. This is the time to say a real goodbye to your marriage and accepting this closure opens a doorway to a new beginning.

Some goodbyes are short, some are long, some are easier and some are harder, but you have to be able to say goodbye to the marriage before you say hello to your future. We know that this is more difficult for some of you than others. Marriage dreams can be hard to abandon. You may even be asking why we have this chapter in here. Well, this is a process that has to happen, as easy or as hard as it may be. Saying goodbye to your marriage and the details that create your picture of that union, takes a bit of reflection. You are saying goodbye to your hopes and dreams and grieving the life that you thought you would be living.

Part of saying goodbye is having the courage to examine the relationship. It's human nature for us to not want to take ownership for our roles in conflict or failure. From the age of two, we learned to say, "I didn't do it." Robbing yourself of growth and healing is denying yourself the ability to not make the same mistakes again. When you see yourself as a victim, you set yourself up to be powerless in changing your future. The only way for you to build your future is to accept responsibility for your past.

For many, goodbyes in society are formal opportunities to assist in the grieving process. When someone we love dies, we have a funeral. When we have milestones in our lives, there are formal celebrations or ceremonies to mark the passing or transition. There are assigned times and specific ways to facilitate saying goodbye. There are no formal ceremonies or opportunities in divorce that help us say goodbye. So, we have to create those for ourselves. You may have already worked through this process. You may be in the middle of this process. Some of you may not have even started the process of truly saying goodbye. Here are a few questions that can help you determine if you have worked through the process of saying goodbye to your marriage. You may choose to answer with a simple "yes" or "no"—but remember, the power of growth and clarity is best if you can share yourself in a complete answer.

- ♦ Can you explain why your marriage ended?
- ♦ Do you understand and accept responsibility for your role in the failure of your marriage?
- ♦ Can you describe why you fell in love with and married your former spouse?
- ♦ Have you made peace with the fact that your marriage is over?
- ♦ Are you ready to let go of the life you shared with your former spouse?

If you answered "yes" to all of these questions, then you are indeed ready to say goodbye to your marriage and embark on a journey toward healing, wholeness and a new life. If you answered "no" to one or more of these questions, then you might have some work to do before you continue working through this book. If you are not sure how to answer some of these questions, then let's explore some of the issues a little further to determine the truthful answer.

It is important that you are able to understand and put into words why your marriage ended. Of course, this does not have to be an objective truth shared by you and your former spouse.

Realistically, most couples never completely agree on what went wrong or see their conflicts from the same perspective. If you could agree on those things, you probably would not have gotten divorced to begin with. However, you must come to your truth—a truth that is honest about your role and choices and an honesty which allows you to tell your divorce story with an explanation that you completely understand and accept. For some of you, there may be answers you will never have, but you have to fill in the blanks to the best of your ability. You must make peace with your story before you can bring it to a close.

It is critical that your story focus, not on the faults, problems and choices of your former spouse, but on your own faults, problems and choices. Of course, we understand that many of you were hurt, betrayed, lied to or even abused in your marriage. We do not want to diminish how you were hurt or wronged, but we firmly believe that there are no blameless victims when a relationship ends. Some people struggle with this. They have been so hurt that it is hard to see past what was done to them. But let's be honest, you cannot change your former spouse. You cannot change anyone except yourself. The power to shape your future lies only in your changes, decisions and choices. Therefore, your story about what went wrong in your marriage should contain a lot of sentences that begin with "I" and few (if any) sentences that begin with "He". If you are not ready to accept responsibility for your role in the end of your marriage, you are not ready to move forward with this book. Set it aside and work on understanding how you contributed to the end of your marriage. This knowledge will empower you to make different choices for your future and take you in a new direction, knowing you will not repeat the mistakes of your past.

A huge part of saying goodbye to your marriage is being able to see and embrace both the good and the bad. For most of us, there are good memories or wonderful experiences that came out of our union with our former spouse. However, the pain of divorce may cloud our ability to see and remember the good things. Goodbyes include acknowledging both the good and the bad, being able to hold on to what was good, redeeming and positive, while saying goodbye to the relationship and its wounds.

It is time to accept the reality that your marriage is over and you will never have it back. You must let go of your former spouse as your husband, lover, friend, partner and family. You will also have to let go of the life and traditions you shared together. You can have treasured memories of the good times, and I hope you do, but you must face the reality that the life you had together is over before you can say goodbye. If you are not ready to do this, that is OK. A counselor or a coach can help you work through the process of getting to the point where you are ready to let go. Perhaps, your divorce is not final and reconciliation is still a realistic possibility. If this is where you are, then you are not ready to focus on your future and re-building your life. You cannot look backward and forward at the same time. You must resolve your questions and concerns about the past and close that door, so that you can fully focus on moving forward. The ability to say goodbye (not yelling it with many flavorful and descriptive choice words proceeding) is one of your first signs of knowing you are ready for renewal!

Think about times in your life (or maybe several) when you remember a bad goodbye. A time when you wish you could have had a do-over. Maybe leaving that situation or person felt so negative; maybe you were filled with anger, sadness, or per-haps you feared the repercussions. You probably had knots in your stomach and throat and thoughts racing in your head, "I should have said this or that" or "I wish I had done this or that differently." Here, our encouragement to saying goodbye to your marriage is this: search and see the value in doing this stage well. Are we suggesting that you drive over to your ex-spouse's home, ring the doorbell, offer a cheery hello and say, "I'm here for us to hug and say our goodbyes with love?" We don't know, that may be the way you choose to work out your goodbye. Some others of you may write a letter followed by watching it burn in the embers and the words for only your reading. Still others of you may choose a completely different route. This is your divorce ritual of releasing what needs to be let go of and holding on to what needs to be held on to. The goodbye we are describing needs to be defined by you. May it bring peace to your soul. A soul that is free to fly.

A Personal Message from Sandra:

Goodbye – there were many of them. In fact, life has a lot to do with saying goodbyes. To me, they feel a lot like surrendering. "Surrender" means to accommodate ourselves to what is beyond our control. This ushers in anxiousness, mixed with some fear, mixed with some losses. But the surrendering allows the goodbye to be mixed with some peace. As we close the chapter of our marriage, there are huge amounts of healing power in reaching the point of acknowledging the memories, grieving hopes and dreams and moving into a goodbye.

It took me a year or so to realize I had to say goodbye to my extended family. No one ever mentioned the value in assessing my losses, nor seeing the ones I had grieved with a peaceful acceptance and moving on. When I focused on the areas of my divorce life that were still causing me pain or discomfort, this one blew me away. I finally admitted that it was very hard to let go of my extended family-by-marriage.

My former mother-in-law was a very dear and wonderful role model for me. She taught me to be a woman and many life skills of being a mom that my own mother had not taught me. Her holiday celebrations were incredible. It wasn't that they were elaborate, but they were filled with so much love for her family. The table was always set so festive (even if it were cute paper plates and plastic silverware). Christmas presents were thoughtfully purchased and were always just that perfect gift wrapped with so much care. Sundays afternoons were reserved for family-time and a meal to share. You truly felt loved from the minute you walked in her home – she had the gift of hospitality. This has had an incredible impact on the way I have created my home and time with my children.

I missed being a part of this family unit. However, after divorce, the ex-daughter-in-law just doesn't fit in the family portrait like before. They still loved me and we had a good func-

tioning "ex" family relationship, but I still had to say goodbye to being the daughter-in-law and all the blessings that surrounded that role.

Another goodbye, I am vulnerably and embarrassingly going to share, was the need for my ex-husband to fulfill my longing for financial security. I didn't want to feel intimately abandoned again; I longed to feel loved and protected. These needs were born when I was five years old upon the message, "You're daddy went to live with Jesus tonight (he was killed in a car accident). My mother didn't know how to successfully navigate the pain, the loss and financial responsibility for two little girls and widowhood. She began using alcohol, prescription drugs and men as her coping skills. I didn't know until later working through my own healing process that my need for a husband to save that scared little five-year-old girl was more than any man should have the responsibility to do. I was looking for a man to be my savior instead of looking to the only One who can be my savior.

Sandra

A Personal Message from Jennifer:
The process of saying "goodbye" is very individual and very personal. For me, the process

of goodbye took over a year. But this process was done in small pieces. I do know that you cannot say goodbye until you have accepted the reality that the relationship is truly over. In North Carolina (the state where my divorce took place) there is a mandatory waiting period of a year between the time a couple physically separates and when they can be divorced. At first, I didn't understand the reason for this waiting period. But now, I am clear that this time is helpful on many levels. By the time my divorce was final, I had said my goodbyes. The goodbye process for me meant being able to embrace and accept both the good and bad of the relationship. It also meant working to see the relationship clearly. I worked to understand why the two of us came together, why we chose to make the commitment of marriage and the how and why of where things went wrong. The most important thing I learned in the process of saying goodbye to my marriage was that the answers I was seeking and the understanding I needed could only come from inside me. Like many women, there was a time when I looked to my ex-husband for the how and why answers. That process was confusing and frustrating. If two people had the same perspective on the relationship and could communicate effec-tively, a divorce would likely not happen. Part of accepting the divorce is finding the answers you need about your decisions and choices and perhaps, accepting that you may never fully understand your spouse's decisions and choices. As a counselor and coach, I often work with people facing grief. Whether your grief is the result of a divorce, a death or another situation, people often don't get the "goodbye" they are hoping for. Some do not get to say goodbye while the person is alive. Closure often comes from an internal journey, not from hearing what you need from another person.

Usually, saying goodbye includes some type of forgiveness. That was a large part of my goodbye process. Unlike some people, I did get a type of apology from my ex-husband. He actually said the words, "I'm sorry". But I didn't get the apology I needed. I had to work through the process of forgiveness anyway. I highly recommend a good Christian counselor to help you work through some of the more significant issues of forgiveness and grief. I had two wonderful counselors over a seven year period during and following my divorce. The goodbye process can take time and it is not easy, but you must be intentional about the process. Time does not heal all wounds without focused and intentional choices to face into the pain and reality of the loss. But if you put in the time, effort and work, you will reap tremendous rewards. The pain does end. New life is possible. Every ending does hold the promise of a new beginning, as cliché as it may sound. But you must take the steps to move forward each and every day.

Jennifer

YOUR TRANSFORMATION

Write a letter to the parts of your divorce you need to say goodbye to. You may or may not choose to send this letter—that is a personal decision. Attached is a letter from Sandra's personal journal dated July 2000. The letter was never sent, but was transformational in her life.

Dear Ex,

I have not had many good thoughts about you or our marriage over the past year. The pain and nasty words and accusations about me caused me to build a brick barricade around my heart and memories. But today, I was walking to my car and I heard birds chirping and the air had the feel of spring. It reminded me of Easter at my grandmother's house. I smiled. That felt really good.

I wasn't expecting the tears that followed, but they also felt good. Through the runny nose and "my ugly cry", so much was released. I'm not mad anymore. Today, I can say I failed you—you failed me—but living in that hateful place isn't working for me anymore. We are two fallible people. I accept that now. I'm letting go of this toxicity—I want to smile and enjoy my days.

"Forgiveness is not the misguided act

of condoning irresponsible, hurtful behavior.

Nor is it a superficial turning of the other cheek

that leaves us feeling victimized and martyred.

Rather it is the finishing of old business and allows

us to experience the present,

free of the contamination from the past."

By Joan Borysenko

Chapter 3

• • •

Packing Up Your Divorce

• • •

Getting Ready to MOVE?

The word "move" immediately makes us think about relocating from one place to live to another; or moving from one business location to another. Just the thought of moving conjures up feelings of how the process is overwhelming, tiring and going to be a whole lot of work. It takes planning, organizing, packing, and unpacking; but it is also a good time to de-clutter. When you move, you will take an inventory of your possessions to see what is of value to keep and what is best to let go of. You will identify items that will be stored away for safe keeping, discard unwanted items, perhaps have a garage sale, and begin thinking about how things will fit into your new place.

It is time to move out of your divorce and into the rest of your life. Let's get moving, girlfriend...

In this chapter, we will reference the divorce process as the "legal dissolution" part of your marriage. Just like your marriage, the circumstances wrapped around your divorce varied for each of us.

- ♦ You may have had an amicable separation and divorce.
- ♦ You may have hired the "best" attorney in town.
- ♦ You may have been able to do mediation.
- ♦ You may have fought your dissolution out in court.

Your circumstance may be highlighted above or may be completely unique to you. Whatever processes you went through, the fact is you are now divorced or on your way to being divorced. This is your reality, and you cannot embrace your future if you are still holding on to the past. Just like the caterpillar who takes up residence in a cocoon; a transformation needs to take place. A part of your past is now intertwined with your divorce process. This is important to discuss because it has played a key role in how you went from being married to being single. You will take an inventory of your divorce process and see what needs to be discarded and what needs to be stored away for safe-keeping.

You may be thinking you really don't want to read or work through this chapter, and honestly we understand. Reliving your divorce experience is never a pleasant experience. Trust us on this one: you absolutely must "work through" this chapter, both through this book and in your life. If part of your conversations (venting) are still traveling back to your divorce, you will need to take extra time here before you are ready to read on. *What we mean by this statement is: if you are still unloading your emotional baggage on others about what you did or did not receive in your settlement, what your ex-spouse is or isn't doing or are expending much of your energy and time on retelling your divorce story– you need some help to pack up your divorce process.* Again, we are not debating whether you were treated fairly in the process (should have received more or less of...), but are positive this can keep you stuck in your divorce for as long as you give it the power to do so. Step outside of your divorce and see how it is impacting you, your family and your life. Maybe consider asking someone you trust to have this evaluation discussion with you.

Divorce is one of the most painful and life altering experiences in life. It is never the hope or wish when two people pledge their commitments, love and futures together. You trust one another and begin living as "one" in the most intimate relationship you have. Sharing yourselves intimately, your children, your home, your finances, your dreams and then one day one or both of you says, "it just isn't working anymore." "Separation" almost seems like a clean word for the ripping and tearing that goes on from that moment on. This process comes with a high price tag emotionally, financially, and physically for everyone involved.

Some women almost sleep walk through their days, while others allow anger to propel them, and others choose denial of their reality. No matter which approach is taken, most women agree they did not recognize the person they became during the early stages of their divorce.

All of us need safe people and forums for venting when life presents challenges. Some women recruit a posse of supporters to relieve their own anxiety and fears, but go on to add in too much of the dirty laundry and camp out with their divorce story. If you are one of these women, you need to know that this is a temporary fix. In the end, you and your ex-spouse are the ones who must live out your divorce obstacles and options. This may be hard for some of you to read, but remember two things here: you cannot change what you do not acknowledge; and the truth does have the power to set you free. Read John 8:32 *("Then you will know the truth, and the truth will set you free.")*

It almost seems as if it is our DNA makeup and especially true of us women, when divorce is going to happen, we begin venting. It doesn't make you a bad person for telling your story, but our goal here is to move beyond this place so you are no longer stuck in your divorce. We are generally more emotional as women, and if we're honest, we just want to hear validation that we will survive and we aren't to blame. Just be aware that these venting sessions can be uncontrolled and can be extremely damaging, particularly when children are involved. During this "fog" time, our emotions conduct the information train and we say what-ever we are thinking at that moment.

We are discussing living in the divorce process – again this refers to the parts of your life you never dreamed you would be dealing with, such as: co-parenting schedules and how to share to the holi-days, decision-making for your children, division of your assets and debts, whose name is on which credit card or auto loan, selling or not selling the home, dividing the living room furniture, future support and so on. While working in the legal system, is it quite hard to begin moving forward. You have to stay in a negative place to fight, be angry, file ongoing lawsuits—which all take so much energy, money and time. To figure out much of this, people enter into a mentality that is all-consuming but also breeds anger and bitterness. Words are hurled at one another through phone calls, emails, texts and via letters from attorneys; then, there are the helpful friends or family members whom like to be what we call "pot-stirrers" and want to keep reminding you of a list of your ex's wrong doings or offering up new ones. As long as you attach to this part of your divorce, you will not be able to begin putting your life back together. It is a huge hurdle to move forward if you are still attached to the divorce process and your past. This stage robs children of their mommies, friends of their friends, employers of their employees, God of his daughters, and you of yourself. It takes so much negative energy to stay in this place.

If you are tired of this battle then you are ready to take a serious look at what needs to be finished up and let go of what is finished. The transformation exercise below will help you put together your action plan for doing this.

Tossing out feels freeing and energizing. It makes room for the "new ___". So now it is time to start packing, my friend. Your future is calling.

A Personal Message from Sandra:

For 12 years now, I have been a divorce mediator and have worked with over 500 divorcing couples. I believe I have a few observations to share. The new wounds created during and by the actual divorcing process are almost as damaging as the wounds of reason that lead to the divorce in the first place.

Just because the papers are signed doesn't mean you are finished with the process until you decide it is finished. There can be years lost in analyzing whether the settlement was fair, whether the process was done correctly, and on and on. People sometimes believe they should have gone for "more" of something or "less" of something, from time with the children, money or household goods. They wonder if they should go visit their attorney again to rehash how things went in the process or maybe hire another attorney to see if the case will be resolved differently with another Judge.

The "maybes" and "should haves" will lock you into your divorce as long as you allow them to do so. Have you asked yourself if it is time to move on over to acceptance and see what you need to learn from this process and what you need to surrender? Unfair as it may be, this is your reality. I was no different for a period of time – I wanted my attorney to win for me the security of my financial future so my children and I would be just fine. After a lot of money and wasted time, I had to accept my reality for what it was and I had to take responsibility for what I would do with my future options. Only in acceptance of my reality did I receive the gift to be free to move on. I didn't agree with or necessarily believe everything was fair in the separation agreement, but more importantly, I didn't like the person I had become in the process.

I would like to add in another important point here. Remember the phrase "fair is in the eye of the beholder"? There is no universal "fair". Also, no two couples are the same – so comparing your situation to a friend-of-a-friend, or your sister's divorce or you name the person, isn't beneficial. They don't have the same financial situations, faults, no faults, children, needs. People compare pieces of their married life and others respond with their opinions about what you should or shouldn't get. This can be a very costly mistake. If you are still making this one, I encourage you to stop and take a deep look at your whole picture and not compare unless it is exactly the same as yours.

I am often asked the question, "How can you hear, watch and work with people going through divorce without living in a saddened and depressed state?" My response is always the same: It does sadden me, but it doesn't depress me at all. In fact, I am so proud of the couple that has the ability and courage to choose mediation over their other divorce process options. There is no one better to decide how to raise the children they love, financially support the children they are responsible for or work through the business affairs of their married life than the two that created it all. They just need to know their legal rights and work with the right professionals to help them achieve a settlement. I have discovered that most people can live with the outcome as long as they felt they had the chance to be heard regarding their opinions and choices, and have the education to speak regarding the decision that needed to be reached. They can then go on and live with the resolution better than when attorneys or judges decide the dissolution for them. Especially when there are children involved, couples need guidance on how to redefine their relationship and work together. At the end of the day, the professionals will all go home; it is the couple who has to do this for many, many years to come.

Divorce must simply be approached differently than the system and manner to which we have all come accustomed to. If the marriage has failed, people need closure and need to be able to move on and begin the journey to healing. If children are involved, they need their mommy and daddy. They need to feel loved, cherished and provided in their emotional, physical and spiritual growth. They do not need to choose between their parents or be responsible for how well their parents are going through the divorce process. I heard Dr. Phil once discuss how divorcing parents should put an invisible fence around their divorcing issues; a fence around their co-parenting relationship; and a fence around their emotional issues from the divorce and not allow the issues to jump into the other yards. This has been a powerful visual statement that I offer when working in my mediations. Dr. Arch Bald Hart, in his book The Anxiety Cure, speaks of the fact the adults are the ones getting the divorce and divorcing one another – not their children.

Even as a Christian mediator, it is not my role to validate whether or not the couple should be divorcing. I come into their lives after the couple has already made the decision to divorce. This process is a kinder and a more gentle approach to divorce as the parties hold the responsibility for how the resolution is crafted. Today, as I write this, I am thrilled to share that approximately 15% of my clients choose to stop mediation and return to working on the marriage union. I believe this style of mediation allows people to listen to what the other is saying and it is no longer a bunch of accusations and threats without serious consequences. When people are splitting their money and their children's time – consequences are very real.

I also know that this time in people's lives can be very destructive and oftentimes holds them in limbo. The energy it takes to stay angry, locked in the past, or living in fear of your future is exhausting. The sooner the parties resolve their divorce negotiations, the sooner they can move forward into the next chapter of their lives. Today, I hope your "win" isn't in the legal process, but in how you will live. If you have children, I hope the same for them.

Blessings as you start packing up and moving on.

Sandra

A Personal Message from Jennifer:
If there is one part of my divorce process where I made the most mistakes, it would be here. I cannot tell you how important it is to attend to the legal details of your divorce quickly and

with guidance and advice from good legal professionals who do not have an emotional investment in your marriage or the fact that it is over. I say this because I fully understand that as women, it can be challenging to separate our feelings and emotional response to our marriage, and the fact that it is over, from the legal aspects of the divorce. I was so overwhelmed with the emotional, spiritual and relational issues surrounding the end of my marriage that I paid very little attention to the legal aspects. My ex-husband and I went through mediation. I did not hire a divorce coach (at the time - I wasn't aware there were divorce coaches) and I did not hire an attorney to protect my interests or give me legal advice. My husband filed for divorce and I simply signed the papers I was asked to sign. In short, the results were devastating to me emotionally, legally and financially. Somehow, I thought taking an active role in the legal process of my divorce would make me more spiritually responsible. This was very untrue and a terrible mistake. Whether or not you want the divorce, you must take responsibility for making good legal and financial choices for yourself and your children. You must find people to help you think clearly and make good decisions in the midst of your emotional turmoil. I find that many women and men avoid taking an active role in the legal aspects of their divorce because of a fear of conflict. Avoiding conflict rarely solves problems and generally causes more problems. Many women allow strong emotion (pain, anger, resentment) to cloud their judgment and make them reactive rather than proactive.

My failure to deal directly and proactively with the legal aspects of my divorce created stress and prevented me from moving forward and building a new life. Make no mistake, you cannot start a new life until you have closure (on all levels) in your old one. But don't confuse saying goodbye (in the previous chapter) with packing up your divorce. Your goodbye process is your journey and on your timetable. Packing up the legal aspects of your divorce is more time relevant. Procrastination in this arena will not likely do you any favors. Allowing your fear to be in control will also work against you. Working through your grief, fear and pain should not be done in a courtroom. Let me give you strong motivation to pack up your divorce: your new life will truly start only when you are able to pack up your divorce and put it behind you.

Jennifer

YOUR TRANSFORMATION

In this exercise you are taking an inventory of your divorce process. This checklist will help you prepare for what belongs in your boxes.

✓ Are you finished with the legal system regarding your divorce?

✓ Do you need to stop saying negative comments about your ex-spouse? Whether or not what you are saying is true, are you sharing with the correct person or venting?

✓ How often does something about your divorce process come up in your conversations? Is it time to pack up some of those conversations?

✓ Are you hanging on to paperwork that fuels hurt and negativity? ("safe-keeping" isn't holding on to pictures of pornography you found on your ex's computer or hurtful correspondence between attorneys).

✓ Do you need to apologize to your children for things they saw or were told during the divorce process? Do they need professional guidance to help with their feelings and emotions surrounding the divorce?

✓ Are there items that were purchased as a couple which need to be sold or given away because of the memories or peaceful existence? (One example: Sandra's kitchen table had become a hurtful place because of some of the damaging fights that occurred. As part of "packing up my divorce", I sold the table. I also vowed that dinnertime would never be a platform for negative or hurtful discussions. I am proud to say that vow has been honored).

✓ Do you need to take care of some outstanding paperwork that keeps circling around you like a black cloud? (i.e. changing life insurance beneficiaries, creating a new will).

✓ Do you need to file away any documents that need to be kept safe but out of your daily viewing? (i.e. separation agreement, divorce decree, joint taxes).

✓ Do you need to stop the flow of information coming from well-meaning friends regarding your ex?

✓ Do you need to stop seeking answers to questions that simply won't ever get answered or can you trust the answer if you receive it? (i.e. did you really love me?, wasn't I good enough for you?, why did you want to hurt me?).

✓ What do you need to pack away for your children to have one day?

✓ Are you finished reviewing your divorce through the grid of "fair"? (fair settlement, fair treatment, fair for past hurts)

Trash:
- ✓ Pictures of your ex with another woman
- ✓ Phone records
- ✓ Hurtful letters from spouse or attorneys
- ✓ Anything that brings negative thoughts into your life
- ✓ Things that you no longer need to keep

Store away for later:
- ✓ Memories such as wedding photos (may want for the children one day) or you just aren't ready to get rid of but don't want to throw away
- ✓ Jewelry or other gifts received
- ✓ Cards written between the two of you that you may once want to share with your children as a witness to the love their parents once shared.

File cabinet:
- ✓ You file away your divorce decree
- ✓ Separation Agreements
- ✓ Parenting Plans
- ✓ Legal documents you need to hold onto such as life insurance policies

To do in the next 30 days:

Review your divorce process. What unfinished business do you have to take care of? Do you need to change your beneficiaries, move funds allotted to you in your divorce, re-do your will, retrieve your file from your attorney, close your account with your attorney, meet with an accountant/ financial planner to design a financial plan of action as a single woman? Do you need to return some property or divide property up with your ex? Remove items from around the home that aren't productive.

St. Theresa's Prayer

May today there be peace within.

May you trust God that you are exactly where you are meant to be.

May you not forget the infinite possibilities that are born of faith.

May you use those gifts that you have received and pass on the

love that has been given to you.

May you be content knowing you are a child of God.

Let His presence settle into your bones, and allow

your soul the freedom to sing,

dance, praise and love.

It is there for each and every one of you.

Amen.

Chapter 4

●   ●   ●

Invisible Prison Walls

●   ●   ●

Certainly none of us would voluntarily choose to commit our lives to living in a prison. Absolutely not, of course not, what a crazy thought; but how many of us live within invisible prison walls? Due to some of our life experiences and coping strategies learned through them, we unintentionally build walls that bind us in our own prison. Have you charged and sentenced yourself through some of these strategies: fear, guilt, regret, grudges, excuses, blaming, denial, and shame? They can be your 8x8 cell and a great hindrance to you in the ability to move forward. They allow you to only live tied to the past and prohibit you from looking toward your new future. For healing and growth to occur, the walls must be torn down, one cinder block at a time. Yes, they may have worked initially, but all of these strategies can become destructive if they aren't channeled correctly or eliminated totally. Turning over your responsibilities and actions to them will lock you up quickly into the confinements of a victim role. Change and rebuilding will be elusive. Break free from your cocoon and limit self-destructive thinking and behavior. Be open to setting free the parts of yourself being held in negative space. Don't compromise your energy, time or emotional health. This is your life—not a dress rehearsal. There are no "do-overs." Grab your sledge hammer, my friend, you may have some hard work to do. Start living powerfully and presently in the now.

Fear

The goal of fear is to make us afraid of the unknown. It is a powerful emotion that creates an anxious state in which we make a conscious choice(s) on impulse to help redefine who we want to be in the world. Fear wants answers immediately; to reduce the anxiety. Fear isn't necessarily too concerned with how healthy the choice of resolve is that we take to get our control back. "By all means," fear says, "take it, buy it, eat it, drink it – just do whatever it takes to stop me."

Fear is a natural human response we all share in from time to time. The question for you is not whether you will allow fear in your life, but rather what you will do with it when it shows up. Some fear is "good fear" if channeled in the direction of protection and energy to take a different action. However, all too often, fear breeds feelings of hopelessness, helplessness and negative thoughts. It multiplies quickly from "a single fear" to many fears. Continuing to live in a state of fear will consume your ability to make wise choices. Fear can be the culprit of stalling so many of your hopes and dreams.

YOUR TRANSFORMATION

Identify your fears. After you have identified the fears that are living in your life, then write 2 options and 2 obstacles for each of them.

My fears:

Options: *1)*

            2)

Obstacles: *1)*

            2)

How will you conquer your fears? How will you learn to walk with them and not allow them to

be in control? Now as your fear creeps in, identify the fear, speak to it, call it by name and tell it what value it offers or what and how you will allow this specific fear to be in your day.

Guilt

Guilt is a feeling of remorse that arises when you have done something wrong or think you have let someone down. Now, not all guilt is bad. Emotions, such as guilt, are essential to have social relationships and they motivate people to take other people's feelings into account.

Guilt is ineffective when it is all consuming and paralyzing. If you simply live in a guilty state it is not beneficial and can be quite detrimental. However, there is a time when guilt is advantageous if you allow it to move you into reflective questioning of actions:

- ◆ I feel guilty about my divorce.
- ◆ I feel guilty about my children having to go through divorce.
- ◆ I feel guilty about hurting my ex-spouse, my children, and my family and extended family.
- ◆ I feel guilty as a Christian.
- ◆ I feel guilty that I can't find employment.
- ◆ I feel guilty that I/my children have to leave the home and move.

♦ I feel guilty about my angry thoughts.
♦ I feel guilty that I/we can't go on vacation.

Given any room, most women are great at covering themselves up with guilt. We can't ignore the long-term impact that our choices have on others or the long-term impact other's choices have on us. But there are times when guilt ceases to serve any purpose.

YOUR TRANSFORMATION
Complete the following statements:
I feel guilty about...

I feel guilty about...

I feel guilty about...

Identify with your guilt. What purpose does it have?

Now, what action step can you take to effectively deal with your guilt (i.e. offer forgiveness to yourself or someone else, make a plan for your budget, meet with a coach, counselor, pastor, etc.)?

By each action put a date for accountability when you will be proactive in dealing with your guilt.

Regret

Go ahead, no one else is listening or judging, except you. Right now, in the safe place of you, your book and pen, write out your regrets. Not for one minute will these be easy on your heart. Tears may show up soon, welcome them; they have a role in this as well.

Regrets tend to lose at least some, if not all, of their negative strings which are tugging on your heart and your thoughts. This will happen when they are given a place to live permanently, not with you, but verbally released in a journal or passed on to your coach, therapist, pastor, or even just cried out in your car.

YOUR TRANSFORMATION

What do you regret?

Why do you regret it?

How will you work through and release your regret?

Grudges

Grudges are defined as strongly-held resentment about another person's actions, words or behaviors that don't get resolved amicably. A grudge provides a built-in excuse and can almost dismiss your pain and misery by holding your ex, or situation and/or others accountable. Holding a grudge can be dangerous if you don't find resolution.

In the grid of rights and wrongs, you may absolutely have a right to hold a grudge. However, if you don't find a way to resolve it, then it has the power to destroy your peace and joy. You must find a constructive way to release grudges or they will inhibit your growth and prevent you from moving forward in your life. The real power is in letting grudges go, not in holding on to them. Grudges look for hurt, angry and powerless souls to reside in, feeding on negativity and gossip. There is no room to let beauty in if you are full of negatives.

YOUR TRANSFORMATION
Who/what are you holding a grudge for?

How will you begin working through your grudge(s)?

I choose to allow myself to release this grudge on this date:

Excuses

Excuses are not your friends, they are your enablers. Which excuses do you have for not living a life that reflects hope, joy, honesty and alignment with your values? Just the word "excuse" causes immediate defensiveness and polluting thoughts. They are truly invisible prison walls surrounding our days and actions.

If you are serious about living your life and not your divorce story, you must be committed to truth. Emotional excuses have to be checked at the door by looking at what your feelings are truly saying. We build excuses to protect our positions or situations and ultimately they either keep us stuck or set us free. Excuses can protect us from dealing with our own reality or life circumstances. They live because we choose to keep them alive and active. They are a temporary solution that victimizes a situation and life. To move beyond, first you must acknowledge the excuses surrounding you and then identify options and obstacles.

YOUR TRANSFORMATION

Discuss your excuses with yourself (i.e. my parent is an alcoholic, so therefore I drink; I don't have any money, so why should I budget? I am single now, so why should I go to church alone?).

Do you spend time and energy collecting evidence to support your excuses?

How will you disarm them and the situations that create them?

Do you spend time with friends that enable your excuses?

Once you have found your motivation, the next step is to get rid of any excuses that stand in your way. Excuses allow you to continue living the way you are now without making any tough choices. They let you feel better about not doing things you know you should. In order to live forward, you have to adopt a "no tolerance" policy for excuses. In the end, overcoming excuses is freeing. Instead of wasting time and energy trying to come up with reasons why you can't, you start to see your days, choices, and decisions with increased clarity of how you CAN. You become an active participant in your own life.

YOUR TRANSFORMATION
Eliminating the Excuse Factor: Simple but powerful steps to turn desire into action!

1. Make a plan
2. Organize your process
3. Create a vision with motivations and accountability

Blaming

Blame is a potent and debilitating crutch when it is used towards someone for an action that affected your life and circumstances. Now we are not suggesting that your ex and/or others are not at fault and deserving of blame, but continuing to focus on it is toxic and will not be productive to growth. Toxic blame keeps you stuck in a power-less and victim role because you cannot change someone else; you can only change yourself. This ownership is amazingly freeing! As long as we make it all about divorce or our ex-spouse, it will continually rob us of power to change the out-come. Set yourself free!

YOUR TRANSFORMATION

How is blame helping you grow into the woman you wish to be?

How is blame giving the other person all of the power (remember you cannot change someone; only yourself)?

How is blame keeping you stuck in being the woman you don't wish to be?

It is vital to understand the culprit of your blame, its role in your existence, and how it hasn't produced a positive outcome for you. The first challenge is confronting and taking the next steps to wholesome resolution. If there is no resolve at this stage, then seek guidance on which is the best next step to take to have the healthiest and wisest outcome for you. Do what you can to understand your role in the situation, seek the best resolution, and then get rid of the blame by dropping it off somewhere. Do not choose to allow it to take a seat in your life and future.

Denial

Oh, the comfort of denial. In his book, <u>Healing from Damaged Emotions</u>, David A. Seamands says, "The correcting of injustices and unfairness and the hurts of this world is God's business and He warns, 'Keep out of my business!'" Denied problems take refuge underground and then take root in sabotaging any truth which must be recognized in order for there to be a chance of growth. Facing the issue, the injustice, the pain, will take audacity, but you are on the road to courageous living. Painful memories, bad decisions and wrong choices have impacted your life at some point, especially in a divorce. The healing and ability to thrive in your life requires breaking through defenses such as denial.

YOUR TRANSFORMATION
Take a deep look at your life, searching far beyond the surface.

Take a walk and reflect on your divorce.

Have a conversation with God and ask him to reveal the truth to you.

Are there any areas that you have not acknowledged?

What are the symptoms that have resulted?

Shame

Webster defines shame variously as an "effect, emotion, cognition, state or condition". The roots of this word are thought to derive from an older word meaning to cover, as in covering oneself literally and figuratively, as an expression of shame.

Shame saddens us and we wish women's lives didn't even involve this word as a feeling associated with divorce. So many women seem to have a blanket of shame covering them following their divorce. Oftentimes it has little or nothing to do with the events of their marriage or divorce process, but because of the word and state of divorce as a Christian. Failure is a close kin to shame. However, you must remember two things: 1) failure is not an event or a person, and 2) shame is self-imposed; don't accept this from another person.

Your divorce has not caught God off guard. He still loves you and walks with you. He is your Father. You have a part in God's story, so you cannot "opt out" of your role because of shame or divorce.

YOUR TRANSFORMATION
Describe your shame. Cry it, feel it and allow the chains to loosen.

Describe ways you know of God's love for you.

Revenge/Retaliation

Boy, these words really sting. It is human nature to be defensive or want get back at someone. You can choose to throw stones back to your ex or anyone else who has wronged you—after all, doesn't he (she, they, it) deserve it? If retaliation or revenge is what you desire, you could spend the rest of your life trying to "get even." We can do anything we can think of to make our offender's life miserable or even "hate" them by holding a grudge, as if this will somehow make his/her life unhappy. But in reality—it causes us to get down on the same negative and destructive level as the offender.

God hasn't turned the judgment of our ex, or anyone for that matter, over to us. He appointed civil government to be the administrator of justice. And if the civil government fails us, we still only have the choice to be as active in the resolution option as is healthy for us. We have to be willing to turn the outcome of punishment over to being God's business.

Retaliation and revenge are two of the worst possible ways to handle wrongs of others and hurt. The cycle won't end. Don't allow yourself to continue to pay the high price another day.

YOUR TRANSFORMATION

Reflect on Matthew 5:38-39: "You have heard that it was said, 'Eye for eye and tooth for tooth'. But I tell you, Do not resist an evil person." What does that scripture mean to you?

If you have children, think about a time when you have been the voice of reason on the topic of revenge. If your son hits your daughter, do you tell her to hit him back? No—you explain the virtue of forgiveness. Your children learn that the authority figure (mom) is the one who delivers the punishment. Bridge this into your own adult life. Will you "hit back" or let the authority figure (your Heavenly Father) deliver the punishment?

Journal about what the following phrases mean to you:
  "turn the other cheek"

  "they got what was coming to them"

  "the karma train will make its way back around"

Reflect on Romans 12:17-21 "Do not repay anyone evil for evil. Be careful to do what is right in the eyes of everybody." What are you doing that is "right in the eyes of everybody"?

Fear, guilt, regret, grudges, excuses, blaming, denial, shame ...one, few, all...have been triggered by your divorce in different doses. They are energy depriving and immobilizing in living your life forward. Starting over with hope and a vision will continue to have unnecessary heartaches if these ghostly justifications harbor in your coping skills. Continuing to turn over actions and responsibility to these things will keep you locked into living life as a victim. In <u>When Lovers Are</u> Friends, Merle Shain writes, "There are only two ways to approach life – as a victim or gallant fighter – and you must decide if you want to act or react...a lot of people forget that." Are you going to act or react to life's circumstances? Here is a hammer, dear one. It's time to free yourself of these prison walls.

A Personal Message from Sandra:

As a divorce coach, I have seen a recurrent pattern in women's lives following their divorce. They get lost in their need to be "right" and build their life around the reasons why they cannot move forward. These women often cling to an entitlement that marriage was supposed to have secured. From there, they build excuses upon excuses to protect the reasons why they cannot change their actions or lives. This gravely saddens me to see women give this power over to the effects of divorce. No one benefits from this, but especially the person building the prison wall. These are termites to living a healthy and well-functioning life after divorce. They are enemies of your growth.

Have you ever heard someone say that un-forgiveness is like, "drinking poison and hoping someone else gets sick." That is kind of what it is like for women when they get wrapped up in these walls of shame, guilt, regrets, excuses, denial... They serve no one well. If this is an area you need some help with, please, I encourage you to work through this chapter, seek outside help from a coach or therapist — don't give up. If you do not deal with these areas of your life, they will at some point in time scream for attention. Your choice to listen and be proactive in dealing with <u>*(fill in the blank your denial, shame*</u> <u>*etc.)*</u> *or you will numb the scream once again with another reactive behavior (eating, shopping, drinking, sleeping, sex). Unfortunately, these resolve nothing and now only add to the issues when your old behavior emerges again.*

No doubt this is a tough chapter. The hardest part is admitting that you are struggling with one or more of these negative coping skills. Remember the admission to your need for help in an area(s) of your life that isn't working well is the beginning to growth and rebuilding. You are a courageous woman if you are taking this step. You are no longer settling for "doing life" the same old way, but are choosing to be free from destructive patterns that will hold you back from living the conscious life that brings honor to you as a woman.

Sandra

A Personal Message from Jennifer:
The way I coped with the turmoil of emotions brought on by my divorce was to throw myself into my career. My husband moved out in March of 1998 and three months later, I interviewed for a new job. The job I interviewed for happened to be my dream job. Let me help you understand

that at the time of my divorce, I was not the type of person who embraced my pain. In fact, I did everything I possibly could to avoid the experience of emotional pain. During the process of the breakup of my marriage and my subsequent divorce, I did not miss a single day of work. I didn't call in sick or take a vacation. I did allow myself one day of crying and emotional pain. I chose a holiday, Memorial Day, so as not to affect my productivity with my grieving. The day after that particular Memorial Day, I interviewed for a job with the American Association of Christian Counselors. I got the job. I threw all my energy, time and emotion into that job. I no longer had a husband and didn't have children. My cat was the only living creature who depended on me, and if you are a cat owner, you realize that dependency is pretty flexible. As long as you provide food and water, cats are pretty good and functioning on their own. I took the opportunity to feel the gaping empty spaces in my life with work. But more importantly, my damaged self worth was dependent on my success. I had failed at my marriage, but I had always been successful professionally. My husband didn't love me, but all of my bosses had adored me. I was a great employee and hard worker and that gave me the sense of value, purpose and belonging I so desperately needed. One of the most socially acceptable and hard to confront addictions is work addiction. This is particularly true for those who work in care-giving fields, particularly Christian ministry related fields. You see, it is hard to confront someone about spending too much time and energy serving God and doing good. Of course, there are many paths I could have taken that would have been more destructive than throwing myself into work. But make no mistake, anything you use to cover pain and use to keep you from facing into the truth of emotional pain and loss is still a defense. At some point, you will have to slow down and the pain will still be there. Also, any good thing (including ministry or a dream job) taken to excess can and will become a destructive force in your life. It took a while, five years in fact, for my work-aholism to catch up with me. It took years of stress, lack of sleep, no attention to key personal relationships and a total lack of physical self-care before I had a breakdown. I had started suffering with migraine headaches a few months after I got married in 1994. They got progressively more intense and more frequent over the years. I kept going to doctors, hoping that a doctor would figure out how to make the migraines stop. Between 1998 and 2003, I was working 90 plus hours a week, getting 5-6 hours of sleep per night and traveling almost every week. I had not had a real vacation since 1997. I wanted to continue my lifestyle, but not feel terrible and be sick all the time. In the spring of 2003, my migraines got so severe that I had a migraine every day for 6 months. I could not function without an enormous amount of pain medication. Even with that, I had frequent visits to the local emergency room for IV drugs to stamp out a very severe and debilitating migraine. I finally reached a breaking point where I could no longer function. I took a medical leave from my job and ended up in a hospital in Michigan that specialized in people suffering from severe and chronic migraines. My doctors and other medical professionals taught me that I had a chronic illness for which there is no cure. This shattered my dream that someone would "fix" what was broken so that I could go on and live my life however I pleased. Instead, they taught me that my health and quality of life would depend on my choices. I could make choices to care for my body through getting enough sleep, eating well, exercising and practicing good stress management and self-care. Or, I could continue with my current lifestyle and experience the consequences inherent in those choices. But the more powerful message during this time came from God. He made it clear to me that my value to Him had nothing to do with my performance or any of my "doing". I was just as valuable to Him lying in my hospital bed as doing all the good work I exhausted myself with over the past decade. Through these experiences, I was able to make critical changes in my life. I now consider myself a "recovering workaholic" who has to make choices each day to take care of the one and only physical body God has given me. I make it a priority to get enough sleep, exercise, eat well and, most importantly, to set boundaries that manage stress in my life. Pleasing others is no longer the source of my value and self-worth. This truth has set me free. Whatever your invisible prison walls, at the core is probably some faulty thinking about your value and worth. That was true for me and has been consistently true for all the women I have coached and counseled through the years. Whatever your invisible prison walls are, let me assure you that only you hold the key to your freedom.

Jennifer

Growth is betrayal of arrangements that were...

Growth is change that is threatening

As well as promising...

Growth is denial of something and

Affirmation of something else...

Growth is dangerous and glorious insecurity.

Author unknown

Chapter 5

24 Hours of Intentional Living

Life is created one moment at a time and those moments make up each 24 hours equaling one day and those days are strung together equaling your life. Your ability to understand the impact of each day is one of the most amazing gifts you can offer to yourself. Today is a gift, what will you do with it?

After years of working with divorced women, we have determined that there is a condition called, "divorce fog"; and this often follows many people for years after the divorce papers have been signed. Divorce can have a huge impact on our lives, thoughts, visions and attitude toward life. One of the early steps in our coaching sessions is to discuss the power of living an intentional life, one with clarity and purpose and one that no longer allows divorce to rob a woman of her life. Choose today to surrender—no more coasting through the motions of your days with various activities without connection or relation to your bigger vision for life. An early comment often shared by women is, "I don't see a way to do life any differently." Transitioning from married to single again is difficult. This journey is long and lonely; terrifying at times. We wish we could tell you that is would be as easy as taking a dress back to the department store and saying it didn't fit right – ("Um, yes, my marriage didn't work out so I would like to exchange my life for a new one. Thanks.") It will be challenging, even rocky, and at times you may feel like quitting. But the quality of the life you are rebuilding will be worth the work. Begin watering your life for intentional growth the way you would water a beautiful flower.

A well-lived life is about letting go of the parts that aren't working well, the mindless existing; and fostering new thoughts, attitudes, environments, and choices. It is time to exchange old toxic behaviors for new healthy ones. Through conscious, deliberate action, you can pave the path to a fresh start and a new life you wish to live. Every day you make choices that lead to actions moving you closer to the kind of person you wish to be and the life you desire. You are the CEO of your life. How will you run this company called "Your Life?"

As you have been reading and working through the chapters of this book, you have identified how your divorce is still impacting you. You have started to identify things you need to remove from your life – all in hopes of reclaiming yourself and defining your future. Intentional living will draw you away from just "hoping" and into actually "moving" toward a life of purpose and vision. Choose to stop wasting time on activities and situations that are sucking the life from you. Step back and take an honest look at the areas we are going to cover in the rest of this chapter. We like to refer to this as reviewing the landscape of your life.

Choices

It all begins with a choice. Choices are made from places of fear or freedom. From where do your choices come? We must be willing to take ownership of our choices. Choice involves the evaluation of the cost and the options to determine the best course of action. Choice allows you to live presently and with ability to create your life. It will take you away from focusing on longings and move you into knowing that your future is built by your choices. Choices empower us because we are ultimately the ones that own the consequences and responsibility of them. Do you believe you have a choice in how your next chapter in your life is written? Do you believe you have a choice in the role you will play in your life story? What choices are you making today to guide you into the scenes you wish to star in?

Letting Go

To be able to add more into our lives or move forward, we usually have to let go of one or more things. Can you identify what is preventing you from moving forward in your life (fears, attachments, attitudes, certain beliefs, toxic relationships, areas you identified in Chapter 4 on "Invisible Prison Walls", expectations, perceptions, failed dreams)? What isn't serving you well as you try to rebuild your life after divorce? Are there habits and old thought patterns that you need to let go of so that you can embrace new ones that support you in your new journey? To continue to *emerge victoriously* we ask you to look at what you need to release, write them down and commit to removing these thoughts and feelings from your life.

Attitude

Charles R. Swindoll said, "The longer I live, the more I realize the impact of attitude on life. Attitude, to me, is more important than facts. It is more important than the past, than education, than money, than circumstances, than failures, than successes, than what other people think or say or do. It is more important than appearance, giftedness or skill. It will make or break a company...a church....a home. The remarkable thing is we have a choice every day regarding the attitude we will embrace for that day. We cannot change our past...we cannot change the fact that people will act in a certain way. We cannot change the inevitable. The only thing we can do is play on the one string we have, and that is our attitude...I am convinced that life is 10% what happens to me and 90% how I react to it. And so it is with you... we are in charge of our attitudes." Our attitudes and beliefs have a strong influence over how we live out our lives. Attitudes have everything to do with how we experience life, both in adversity and in joyous times. Positive attitudes are empowering and help us focus on the blessings of each day. We are not talking about pretending to be happy or upbeat all the time. We are talking about a mindfulness that derives from realizing our blessings even in the midst of our sadness, pain and loss.

Our attitudes are a gift we give to ourselves daily. We get to choose our individual approach each and every day.

Developing a positive attitude is a skill that can be learned through intentional living. Attitudes arise from the perceptions we carry about life and living, which is why it is imperative for you to be aware of your perceptions and conclusions about the effects of your divorce experience. It takes tremendous courage to examine the attitudes you hold. What you choose to express in your external life comes from your attitude, which dramatically affects your growth, healing, and ability to achieve a sense of happiness and peace. This is the key to living an intentional, well-lived life.

Begin eliminating negative attitudes and beliefs that contribute to your pain and hopelessness and begin cultivating new and empowering attitudes and beliefs that give you hope. Some examples of negative/positive are: "I am ashamed to be a Christian divorced woman". Now replace that with "I am a divorced Christian woman who is loved and valued by her Father." Another one may be: "I will grow old and be all alone." Stop. Now replace with: "I pray I grow old and live life to the fullest in spite of my circumstances." Think about the negative messages and attitudes you are holding and write them down. Next write a positive affirmation to replace your old thought. Then read these to yourself everyday for the next 30 days. If one is of particular importance, tape it to your bathroom mirror or carry your affirmations in your purse for easy reference. By committing to a removal of negative chatter, you will soon start to believe and live in the positive truth.

The Power of our Thoughts, Self-Talk and other Influences

As we were just explaining above, there is so much power in the messages we say to ourselves. Our choices, decisions and the actions we take all begin with our thoughts. What conversations are you having with yourself? Are they filled with negativity, self-criticism, self-doubt, judgment; or are they filled with encouragement and self-acceptance? Your self-talk makes up your reality and your reality ultimately becomes your attitude. We want you to think about words or phrases that you say to yourself or to others. Write them down and then write a more encouraging word or phrase next to that. Practice doing this as you become more intentional about what you are thinking about and sharing.

> ? *"Because of my divorce, I no longer have enough money to meet my friend for lunch." Now replace that line with: "I have to watch the money I spend, but I value my friendship. I will ask if we can meet for lunch where they offer a buy one entrée and get a second free."*
> ? *"I won't ever get to go on a vacation again since I am alone." Now replace that line with: "I would like to go on a vacation again. I will choose to think about what that would*

*look like and maybe join a travel club or ask
someone to join me on a vacation."*

Begin to actively and intentionally change your
negative thoughts about yourself, your circumstances (including your ex) and in general, all of
the areas that make up your life.

Take Responsibility

You don't have to take responsibility for what
someone else has done. You do have to take
responsibility for your own choices, actions and
attitudes. This is a hard step for most of us. We
see women who get stuck giving away their power
to change the outcome without taking any ownership. They stay victims to their circumstances
and feel they have no choices – to live where they
live, work where they work, or believe their life is
"over' after their divorce.

Are you ready to take responsibility for your
own life, for your health, for your relationship with
your children, for your finances, for your career
and for the life you are rebuilding? Yes, someone
else's decisions may have turned your life upside
down, but don't continue to allow their decision
to rob you of your good memories of your yester-
days, your today, or your future.

Take responsibility for what is yours and let go
of the rest. God can handle the role of judge. Get

in your own backyard and focus on your life. Your integrity and what you do with your life is your responsibility. Remember, you are God's business and your ex or others who have wronged you are God's business. He can take care of His responsibilities. He wants you to be the best you and live the life He has given to you intentionally and to the fullest.

Living Authentically

This is a frightening way to live for some of us women. There is safety behind the masks we wear. We want to be accepted. We want to be admired. We fear rejection and ridicule. So we create another version of ourselves that we believe is better and present that woman in different areas of our lives. Because divorce strips so many beliefs and masks off anyway, why not allow it to strip this one away as well? Be the best "you" and present that self to others. Start getting comfortable with you, learn to like you and to love you. Shed those divorce messages that you may be carrying that were spoken to you and about you. If there are parts of you that you aren't pleased with, then use them to be your guide in making changes.

Authentic individuals listen with their hearts and respond with their eyes and actions. Sometimes it's just a simple eye contact that says a thousand words. Our eyes are indeed the window to our souls. Think about the people you like to surround yourself with – are they genuine and authentic? What is it about their authenticity is that you admire?

"We are what we believe we are." ~ C.S. Lewis

People and Places

Self-reliance is important, but to live intentionally you need to surround yourself with healthy and supportive people and environments. God made us as relational beings. He knew we would need people to walk with us on this life journey. Think about who is on this life journey with you. Are you intentional in fostering and nurturing your healthy relationships? We are the sum of the people who we spend the most time with (this can include the television shows we watch and books we read). After divorce, many women find they lose many of their old friends, their couple friends and extended family members. Making new friends can be a really scary and vulnerable step for most of us as we develop a new support system. This will take time, but now is the time to do so with great intention. We all need people in our lives. We learn from people. Surround yourself with people who are wise because of experience gained; honorable people who are strong in character and who can provide a shoulder for you to lean on when you are tired and weak; and people who can be objective and speak hope, truth and love to you.

Take a look at the people who have influence in your life. What kind of impact are they having on you and your success in rebuilding your life? Relationships that cause discord, stress and pain may need new boundaries or it may even be time to distance yourself from that connection. This is also a great time to think about what kind of friend you are to others. Would you want you for a friend? Living out authenticity is a big step in being a friend and making real connections.

If you are a parent, think about your relationship with each of your children. What kind of story has their parent's divorce written on their hearts and for their future? What are you modeling for them as their mother? It may be time for you to help them write the next chapter in their life as well by the way they see you respond to their father, or the attitude you have toward the divorce and the circumstances it has created. Look for a whole book from us dedicated to this subject. We are passionate about writing it in the next few months.

How is the environment in which you are living? This includes your home, your bedroom, your closet, the inside of your car, your work place, places you choose to go to for entertainment. Our environment affects our attitudes and ability to function well. Do you need to do some un-cluttering, organizing and rearranging? Think about how your attitude shifts if you are trying to get ready for your day or work and all of your clothes are piled on the floor of your closet. Doesn't this set your day off with chaos and a bad attitude? Your marriage and having a spouse wasn't the reason you did the laundry and put it away, cleaned the house, vacuumed out the car, was it? We have worked with women who quit cooking, eating with the children, let the dirty clothes pile up. They take on the attitude that the kids don't care, so why bother. "Bother" because it is your surroundings and they powerfully affect your attitude and energy. Create spaces that inspire you – a closet that is organized so you can find your pants and shirts. Create spaces and views that offer peace.

Gratitude

Dictionary.com defines gratitude as:

a) An appreciative attitude for what one has received

b) A warm or deep appreciation of personal kindness

c) A disposition to express gratefulness by giving thanks

Melody Beattie, author of <u>The Language of Letting Go</u>, writes about gratitude so beautifully. "Gratitude unlocks the fullness of life. It turns what we have into enough, and more. It turns denial into acceptance, chaos to order, confusion to clarity. It can turn a meal into a feast, a house into a home, a stranger into a friend. Gratitude makes sense of our past, brings peace for today, and creates a vision for tomorrow." Wow!

It is hard to be filled with bitterness and anger in the same heart that is filled with gratitude. They just don't co-exist with one another. It just won't work to be thankful for your life while wishing you had a different one. Are you focusing on what you don't have or what you do have? Being thankful for what you have allows you to not get sucked into negativity. Gratitude helps you not to miss opportunities in front of you. Being thankful encourages you to see life through a different lense.

Characteristics of a grateful life:
- ♥ *a sense of purpose in our lives*
- ♥ *an appreciation for the lives of those around us*
- ♥ *a willingness to take action to show the gratitude we feel*

Gratitude is choosing to see God's hand at work in our lives, in spite of our circumstances, and see the evidence of the true and living God around us.

Spirituality

As Christian women, we often carry a heavy bag on our backs filled with shame and guilt. We have sat in church, Bible studies, small groups; we have read books, attended conferences and met with Christian friends and heard the messages of how God hates divorce. We, ourselves, may have shared this message toward others, but now that divorce is a part of our lives we don't know what to do with this message.

The scripture in Malachi is clear: God hates divorce. But throughout the Bible, the scripture is clear about the love God has for His people. He loves you – He hates divorce. Those are different, dear friend. He loves people, He hates sin. Your divorce hasn't taken God by surprise and made Him say, "Well, she is damaged goods and I no longer wish to love her or choose her for my works and glory". He isn't saying that anymore than we would say this to our own children and loved ones.

You may have been wounded by other Christians, and we are sad for that hurt. Have you ever heard the saying, "Christians often shoot their own."? Let's turn to Lamentations 17: 21-22. It says, "Because of the Lord's great love we are not consumed, for his compassions never fail." Do you ever feel like saying the following? "Thank you Lord for knowing how much I would need to hear your words and not only people's." After living with raw emotions, fear and even hysteria at times, do you remember what it means to have someone encourage and support you? Do you know what it feels like to have people be concerned about you and your family? These difficult times don't pay the bills, clean the house, fix the broken microwave, or do earthly tasks for you, but they do offer what your soul longs for. The soul – the connection to the Lord – was filled by His people through difficult and trying times. The encouragement offers you strength to do what you feel you can't, holds on when you don't feel you can hold on any longer, and keeps trying when you fear trying anymore.

Let these tough times resonate with you and never forget how God showed up in His people. Focus on the good God has sent you and not the negatives that others are sending you. Remember to be that same encouragement and vessel for the Lord next time He puts a wounded and hurting life in front of you.

Today, practice living intentionally by:
- ♥ *smiling more*
- ♥ *spending more time enjoying your kids*
- ♥ *being proactive*

♥ *paying attention to others*
♥ *hugging someone*
♥ *journaling what you are thankful for*
♥ *serving someone*
♥ *resolving conflicts*
♥ *laughing*
♥ *limiting complaints*
♥ *breathing deeply*
♥ *speaking words of hope to yourself and others*
♥ *doing one thing to your environment that makes you feel better*
♥ *nurturing your relationship with God and His word*
♥ *listening to uplifting music*
♥ *reaching out and try to make a new friend*

Divorce wasn't a part of your life movie. Your world has changed and your path has been forever altered. As you are rebuilding your life, pray to be self-aware and live consciously. You don't want to come to the end of your time on earth and look back with regrets. You have today – the 24 hours in front of you. Will you choose to live it intentionally and with honor for the blessing it is? Today will soon be gone. It makes up a page in your life; live it as importantly as though it is your last day on this earth.

A Personal Message from Sandra:

When I started my own journey to rebuild after divorce, I knew I wanted to live an intentional life. I had already wasted so many of my days trying to make life work. When I found myself at the end of my rope and no longer had the control or strength to continue, I cried out to God and asked Him to take over. I was finished doing His job. Divorce had stripped me of my many false masks that pride and fear had designed so eloquently for me to wear.

Some people in my life weren't supportive of me through or on the other side of my divorce. I had to be intentional in the role they would continue to play in my life and how their words and actions would impact me and my family. I kept praying for the courage and strength to keep walking toward my life vision and believing that God still valued me. I prayed that God didn't think I was no longer of use to Him since I had divorced.

There are so many external influences in our lives. To live intentionally, I had to put a grid in place to filter who and what I would choose to allow in my thoughts; and what I would give my energy and time to. I became a lot more selec-

tive of these influences knowing the power they had in my healing and growth.

I remember a woman saying to me, "God teaches us lessons in our pain and won't put more on you than you can handle." Well, I had heard that before, but this time I went straight to God and shared with Him: "Father, I don't want to learn anything else in my life; can you just go ahead and teach other people? I am really good with the education I have received through pain and struggles up to this point." However, after some much needed rest and healing, I can admit the value of the journey. I live more fully each day because I never forget where I have walked. The birth of Emerge Victorious was born out of living intentionally today with all my life lessons in tow.

Sandra

A Personal Message from Jennifer:

My view of what it means to live an intentional life has changed dramatically in the last couple of years. I used to think that intentional living meant having direction and focus. How many of you have a GPS system for your car? If you don't, you have certainly been in a car with someone who has one and you know how they operate.

You program in a destination, be it down the road or across the town or across country, then the GPS system does calculations and gives you directions for the best route to get there as well as an estimate of how long it will take. The key to using a GPS is having a defined destination. Without an address or clearly defined destination - one that is already programmed into the GPS or one that you can program - the device is completely and entirely useless. I often feel the same about my work as a coach. If a client comes to me with no goals, no dreams and no idea of where she wants to go, then how am I supposed to help her get there? Intentional living does have something to do with knowing where you want to go, but if you don't know where you want to go right now, that's OK. After a major life crisis, such as a divorce, it is common for people to feel a bit directionless. They often have to set a new course, new goals, re-work the vision and dreams for their life since the old dream didn't exactly work out as we had hoped and planned. Part of the process of this book will be to help you find your destination. It doesn't have to be a permanent or final destination. After all, GPS systems allow you to change your destination during the trip or even take detours. But if you have no idea where you want to go, you are in for some aim-

less wandering. Following my divorce, I felt like I had been wandering aimlessly for a long time. As many other women who find themselves divorced, I had lost myself in my marriage. I lost sight of what I wanted out of life. I forgot what was important to me. Regaining this vision may take some time and we will discuss vision in upcoming chapters, but once you have vision, you must be very intentional about taking steps to reach your destination. The challenge, especially when rebuilding your life after divorce, is that the distance you have to travel to get to your destination may be great. Rebuilding a life from the ground up isn't quick or easy. There may be large obstacles blocking your path that might require you to take a detour or change your route altogether. The danger that many of us face following our divorce is that we will spend a lot of time attending to the urgent (but not necessarily important) matters demanding our attention without giving any thought to the direction we are going. But I am now discovering that there is an even more insidious danger -not enjoying the journey. I am currently facing one of the most challenging times of my life because my direction and focus are changing. Facing a new crisis in my life, my mother's battle with Alzheimer's, has changed me and my life in ways I could not anticipate. In many ways, this transition has been even more significant than my own divorce. Watching the end of someone's life up close and personal has changed my perspective. I have realized that all of us have the same ultimate destination. No matter what path we take, all of our lives will end. I am starting to realize that my destination is not nearly as critical as the journey itself. Of course, the final destination of heaven is important. For me, that decision was made when I accepted Christ at the age of 16. I don't really have to worry about when my life will end or what my final destination will be. God has me covered on both counts. But the journey is up to me. I am much more concerned about intentional living as a means to enjoying my life and making a positive difference in the world. I want to make sure that I live each day with an eternal perspective. I want to make sure that I live my life as if it were my last. I used to ask myself if I accomplished my goals for the day. Now, I ask myself if I enjoyed my day. Did I spend time with those I love most? Am I contributing something positive to the world? Some of the greatest gifts in the life are not goals to be achieved, but simple pleasures of love, joy and contentment that should be embraced as they come to us along the way. For me, intentional living is about making sure my choices each day reflect the things that will matter most at the end of my life - whether that is today, next week, next year or many years down the road.

Jennifer

Today

• • •

when life settles down...

when I get some rest...

when the kids don't need me so much...

when the kids start back to school...

when I lose some weight...

when I get a job...

when I get the laundry done...

when I meet someone...

when I receive my settlement...

when my ex-husband...

Today, my "when" (as important as it may be) will not rob me of my now,

nor will it stop me from taking action

toward building my new normal and my new life.

"When" is no longer tomorrow, "When" is today.

• • •

By Sandra Dopf-Lee

Chapter 6

• • •

Let's Be Honest

• • •

As little girls most of us could hardly wait to start making changes to our outer beauty. We anxiously anticipated our ears being pierced, the "privilege" of shaving, and then permission to wear a little eye-shadow and blush. These outward milestones are huge for young girls – it means she is well on her way to growing up and looking beautiful. As adults we can laugh and wonder why we didn't see how beautiful we were without those enhancements. But this desire is almost intrinsic of being a girl.

As adult women making changes to our inner beauty rarely invokes the same excitement and anticipation. Rather, it usually brings bouts of intimidation, dread and exhaustion before we even begin the process. Women desire for their lives to be different, unfortunately it is not as easy as choosing between blue and brown eye-shadow. Why do we have to do so much hard work and go so deep into our thoughts, beliefs and values? Our outside appearance; our bodies, are mere shells for storing our real beauty which is our precious souls. The work you are doing is bringing forth the inside out so that you radiate as a woman who has emerged into your own story.

The thoughts of actually writing your next chapter of your life story can be overwhelming and paralyzing. To write anything you have to first have an idea of what you want to say in your message. Yes, it will take introspection, time, energy and the ability to be honest about the reality of your life today as you get ready to design your tomorrows. However if reclaiming your life and future is your goal, you simply must take a look at your assumptions, beliefs, truths, values... as you map out your steps forward in living a life with a mission, vision and purpose.

Divorce may have stripped your confidence and trust. It may have stolen your "normal" so you can no longer rely on it to facilitate your days or your truths. Searching for your "new normal" has begun. In the final pages of "O" magazine each month, Oprah Winfrey writes an editorial column entitled *"What I Know For Sure"*. In these columns, she shares wisdom that is very personal to her. She discusses things she believes and has learned from her own life experience. We are asking you to start writing your own "What I Know for Sure" column. As much as we sometimes wish we were living another life, acknowledging the life you are living is the key to stepping into your future. Emerging begins with being honest about your reality and who you are, what you believe and why you believe it.

Values and Beliefs:

We will work toward writing your own mission and purpose statements and they will be built from your core values and belief systems. Your values and beliefs will hold truth in your life when life changes plans on you. They represent what we really find important in life and surprisingly enough, very few women will find it easy to define exactly what their core values are (i.e. trustworthy, honestly, confident, friendly, compassionate, kind, courageous, outspoken, patience, to name a few, and beliefs (I am valuable, I am loveable, I am forgiven, to name a few). Most of us act our lives out according to our values and beliefs and they guide our behaviors.

Core Values: Divorce usually clouds our core values and behaviors. This is why it is so important to identify them for yourself – then you will know if you are living them out in your single-again life or not. These core values are defined as philosophies or principles that inform both internal conduct as well as your relationship to the external world. This is key in planning for your future. So, we ask you, do you know what values are important in your life? Are your values informing your choices and actions on a daily basis?

To live your intentional life, you must compose your life plan with core values that are essential to who you are and who you want to become. You may already have identified your core values, but if you haven't, now is the time. We are sure you have some idea of values that are important to you, but need to think through them more clearly. If you have no idea what values are unique to you, we encourage you to write down the ones that govern your life or the ones you wish to govern your life. Write them down and beside each one write why it is important to you. Then go a step further and put a check by the ones that you can honestly say you are living according to.

Beliefs: After divorce, women often say that they become unsure of what they even believe anymore. Long held beliefs are questioned and new beliefs are scary to explore.

Beliefs are things you know to be true. If you don't explore your own beliefs you may allow other's beliefs to invade your beliefs and your life. Write down beliefs that are your own and know to be true. Whenever you question your-self you can reflect back on your own defini-tions and words.

Conscious awareness of your personal values and beliefs and is like having a personal compass for your do's and don'ts. They will inspire you as you go about living your life. But, if you are unaware of your beliefs, it will cause unrest in your soul. This is because values are intrinsic, ingrained and invisible (until they are surfaced). This tension and confusion can make intelligent actions, let alone informed decisions, nearly impossible. This results in living a life in conflict.

Celebrate where your values and beliefs are true and recognizable in your life. Continue to grow and make choices that will close the gap between your values and beliefs and your daily choices and decisions.

YOUR TRANSFORMATION
Write your own column regarding "what you know for sure" and include your core values and beliefs.

Priorities:

Do you feel like there are not enough hours in the day? Do you feel like you never accomplish the tasks or goals you set out for yourself that you know are most important? If you are ending each day feeling discouraged you may want to evaluate your priorities.

We have a limited amount of time in our lives. There is a saying that is really a misnomer, "you need to manage your time better". The truth is, we cannot manage the time — there is 24 hours in a day, but we can manage ourselves better and how we use the time that is allotted to us. To do this, we have to prioritize what is important to us and our family in retrospect to moving closer to our goals. That goal can be just spending more time with your children or could be securing a job. The priorities and goals belong uniquely to you.

It is vital to be able to set priorities in life — for your days, your weeks, your years, and your seasons of life. Otherwise there will always be a crisis or a need that arises that is more than happy to grab your focus and your time. There will never be enough time to all things — even if they are all "good" things. This chapter is all about helping you decide what is important to you and this will help you with setting your priorities.

"Yes and No" / Boundaries

Christian women are notorious for doing too much and not being able to say "no". We often struggle to set boundaries. A fantastic book we (Jennifer and Sandra) recommend on this topic is Boundaries, by Henry Cloud and John Townsend. In short, boundaries are the lines that separate us from others. They define what our responsibilities are and are not. Healthy boundaries help us take ownership of our lives and treat others with kindness and respect while allowing us to say "yes" to what we want to say "yes" to and "no" to what we want to say "no" to. Do you find yourself agreeing to something and then wishing you were able to say no? Do you feel like a doormat that others take advantage of? Do you have a hard time expressing your views or standing up for what you believe? Then it is time to learn more about boundaries and challenge yourself to set better ones based on what you are discovering about yourself and the life story you are writing.

YOUR TRANSFORMATION

Make a list of "yes" and "no" for your life. On the "yes" list - put things that are important to

you. Don't limit the list to the "big" things (God, your children, your health) but also include small things that you want in your life (the beach, your pet, great shoes, ice cream). On the "no" list, put things, people or feelings you wish to eliminate from your life. Again, not just big things (guilt, shame, people who are not supportive) but small things that create frustration or disharmony in your life (a long commute to work, the sofa your ex picked out).

Get a Life

As we are writing this book, one of our assistants (in the midst of a divorce herself) made this comment, "Sure, I can come by anytime to finish up this chapter. I have no life." Can you identify with this statement? It is a common feeling for women after divorce. Even if you are very busy with the daily activities of life, it can feel as though you don't have a life. What do we mean by this? It means there is nothing we feel passionate or excited about. Having a life means you have thing to do that bring you joy, excitement and fulfillment. It means you seldom get down about your life because you have a zest for your life and a passion for... Well, you have to fill in the blank as it is defined for you. You may find that passion and zest for life through your spiritual life, family, career, hobbies – what infuses your life with passion.

Certainly, there are limits to what you may be able to do due to constraints of time and money (yes, we many of us would like to travel the world or live in Paris for a year), but perhaps you can adapt your passions to something that is achievable in your life today. If you can't get to Paris, maybe you can learn French or take a class on "The Art of the Louvre". We are just encouraging you to live – to thrive and not settle for survival.

YOUR TRANSFORMATION
Make a "bucket list" of things you want to do, places you want to visit, and goals you want to accomplish before you go home to the Kingdom of God.

Clarity:
Most of us struggle with seeing ourselves clearly. Typically, people fall into one of two categories in regard to lack of clarity. Some of us believe we are responsible for everything that happens to us. We are usually very hard on ourselves and are reluctant to be seen as a victim. We do not want sympathy from others and definitely don't want pity. We often evaluate ourselves more harshly than others would. These people generally have an internal locus of control. If you fall in this category, your challenge will be to give yourself a break and not be so self-critical.

Others tend to feel that much of their life is out of their control. They do not take on responsibility for the world, but rather often feel powerless to have great effect on the world or even their own lives. These people can tend to fall into a "victim" role and believe that when bad things happen in their lives, it is bad luck or unfortunate circumstances, but fail to take responsibility for what they do control in their life. These people tend to have an external locus of control. If this sounds like you, your challenge will be to stop blaming your ex-spouse (or others) for the problems in your life and decide what you can do to change things. You may need to reflect back on the chapter "Invisible Prison Walls".

Take some time for self-evaluation. We want you take a good look at yourself and every aspect of your life at this moment for clarity. Where do you stand and how would you rate yourself in each area? You should not try to find an external measurement or give an evaluation of what others might think of you. Remember, this is your truth, not the truth of others.

We, Sandra and Jennifer, recommend watching the movie "Runaway Bride". Even if you have seen the movie before - watch it again. Compare yourself to the lead character, Maggie Carpenter. Are there any ways that you can identify with her? In what ways, if any, have you comprised your desires, beliefs and values for those of your former spouse or other people in your life (i.e. your parents, your boss, your friends)? Journal about the ways you may need to discover or re-discover who you are.

YOUR TRANSFORMATION

Evaluate where your life is today in each of the following categories using a scale of 1-10 (1 being the worst and 10 being the best - exactly where you want to be). This is your grid to know where you need to focus your growth.

1. **Identity/Self Worth - How do you feel about yourself? This is an overall evaluation of where your life is and who you are as a person.**

2. **Career/Employment - Are you working? Are you happy with your job? Are you doing something fulfilling? Does it meet your financial needs?**

3. **Relationships - This can be relationships with friends, family, your former spouse or others. You may need to evaluate different relationships with a different rating, but give yourself an overall evaluation for your support system. We would like to define "healthy relationships" as relationships in which you feel safe and can be yourself**

without fear or pretense. These are relationships that can offer support without judgment.

4. Parenting - If you have children, this would include how you feel about your skills as a parent, your relationship with your children and your co-parenting relationship with your former spouse.

5. Home - This includes the place where you live, environment and surroundings as well as the location and the "feeling" of home.

6. Health - This includes both your physical health and mental health. Evaluate how you feel, your stress levels, your diet and your levels of stress and ability to manage stress.

7. Spirituality/Faith - Where is your relationship with God right now? Be honest. Often divorce can challenge our faith, our views of God and can certainly make us question or re-evaluate what we believe and why. What about your relationship with your church or community of faith? It is possible there have been some changes or challenges there as well? It's perfectly fine to

be questioning and changing in this area of your life right now, but it is also important to face it openly and honestly.

8. **Passion/Pleasure/Joy - This is often a neglected category. This category reflects all the things in life that give you pleasure or joy—the things that make life worth living. The reasons you wake up in the morning and push through the difficult times. These are the things, people, activities or events that make your heart leap and your skin tingle. They excite you and give you energy. It is common to find that those going through a divorce have lost touch with the passionate part of themselves. They have forgotten what truly brings them joy and makes them sing. Evaluate where you stand with regard to having passion, pleasure and joy in your life today.**

A Personal Message from Sandra:

My core values include trust. I value trust so much because of the lack of trust I had in the adults in my life as a child. When my father died I was five years of age and my mother was basically incapacitated, I was left to navigate life on my own. Well, there were some other people in my life that were not worthy of being trusted, yet there wasn't an adult to protect me.

So I have always lived out how much I desire for people to trust me and how much I desire for people to reciprocate. This began with my husband and children. When I could not trust my husband this was a huge break down for our marriage. To me, the ability to trust was and is bigger than love, communication – I must be able to trust someone.

I didn't know my values before I got married or some of the blind spots that I saw in my dating relationship would have been more of a deal breaker. However, I hadn't healed and grown out of my childhood dysfunction and learned to see and know how this core value is so important to me and how much I cannot live successfully without it.

Sandra

A Personal Message from Jennifer:
The turning point in my journey toward rebuilding my life after my divorce was when I made the choice to accept responsibility for my part in the failure of my marriage. I certainly had reasons to blame my ex-husband for many things. His

depression, substance abuse, and relationships with other women gave me plenty of excuses to blame him for everything. But I was fortunate enough to have people in my life (professionals and friends) who encouraged me to look at myself and no one else for answers to why my life had gone so wrong. I had to ask myself very difficult and challenging questions. Why did I not see the signs of the problems my ex-husband was dealing while we were dating? Why did I choose to go through with our marriage in spite of significant doubts and fears? I knew there were red flags, why did I choose to ignore them? Why did I ignore the warnings from several of my friends and colleagues of their concerns about the man I was planning to marry? The answers I needed would come from me, no one else. So, the questions had to start with me as well. I learned so much about myself in the process of dealing with my divorce. I had a traumatic event in my life years before I was married that I never dealt with. The result was Post Traumatic Stress Disorder that I kept hidden. It eventually resulted in depression. These issues - and my denial about them - kept me from thinking clearly and making good decisions. My pain led me into a relationship that was inauthentic and all about "not feeling". It was only when my marriage (and subsequently my life) fell apart that I faced these difficult issues and dealt with them head on. I spent time in individual and group counseling. I invested lots of time and money in healing. Let me be honest. It was hard work. It was painful and scary and very uncomfortable. I had to face situations and emotions from my past that I did not want to face. But the only way to heal from the pain of your past and your divorce is to face into the most deep and difficult parts of your life and yourself. This journey is not for the weak or faint of heart. But it is the only road I know for moving your life forward in a positive direction. There is no way around it - only through it. You must start by being honest....at least with yourself.

I want to thank those who walked with me and supported me on my journey:
-My gracious heavenly Father who truly gave me the grace I needed.
-Three wonderful counselors who gave me safety and no judgment (Bev, Linda and Beth).
-Many wonderful friends who have given me unconditional love and support (but especially my dear friend, Richard).
-An angel cat, Teka, who opened my hardened heart and taught me to love again with deep passion.

Jennifer

The Serenity Prayer

●   ●   ●

God grant me the serenity to

Accept the things I cannot change;

Courage to change the things I can;

And Wisdom to know the difference.

●   ●   ●

Author Unknown

Chapter 7

Designing Your Life Vision

Imagine you are standing beside the ocean with waves breaking along the shore, the morning is bright and breezy, and before you is a blank canvas and a palate of paints with all the colors of the rainbow. Take your brush and with each stroke envision your new life picture as you dream of your future.

We know that dreaming a vision for your new life, stroking some colors of paint on canvas, putting some pictures on a board and writing some goals, won't automatically produce the life you desire. It didn't happen for us that way and we haven't heard anyone else reveal that it happened that way for them. However, we must first foresee what it is that we want before you can begin to create a life you choose to live.

These tools will have a significant role in your transformation and helping design your future, but it takes time, work and commitment. The end result is what excites us so much about this chapter. We are not only living testimonies ourselves, but have witnessed it over and over in the lives of many women. W. Clement Stone said, "If we fail to plan, we plan to fail." With the right tools and resources, your purpose, vision and goals defined, you are ready to move forward.

You have probably heard the quote, "Don't opt out of your role in God's story". We know you don't want to "opt out", you may just want to know how to "opt in" to His story as you start over. You may be tired of focusing on the effects of divorce and choose to shift your focus. It is time for a new vision, and in order to make room for it, you will choose to let go of the "old" married vision of life and all the stories that went along with that theme. You are single and you want to live this story well; a life story that is beautiful, graceful, and full of integrity, designed by your purpose, passions, and principles.

When divorced women explain what their "new" life is for themselves, they usually struggle to answer. Yet, without a vision, how can someone even begin to put a road map in place to follow.

You are going down this road, so why not make it one worth traveling? Take the time and effort to map out a course that will give you the end results that you desire.

"Designing Your Life Vision" is a chapter written to guide you as you create a true vision and draw the road map for working toward that life. Having your vision in place will help you decide where you are and where you want to go, your life GPS, and it can only be programmed by you. It begins with a mental picture and then the ability to articulate that picture into defined vision, and then the ability to translate it into your reality. This is retrospective in that you fast forward to visualize your desired life picture; then come back to your reality and identify the plan, goals and actions needed to move you closer to your vision. So we ask you, ladies, are your daily choices and actions leading you closer to the life you wish to live? Is it time to change your yes's and no's and how you are spending your days, weeks, months and years?

What are some words you think of as you prepare for transition? Rebuilding, starting over, fresh start, new beginnings. We believe it is really important for you to name your journey as you emerge victoriously on the other side. It is helpful in speaking clearly about your attitude and decisions.

Having a clear vision and plan is important especially when we start something new (life, job, exercise program, etc.). Your success will increase tenfold. Let's spend some time together discussing and working through this overwhelming, but powerful chapter. There are a lot of transformational questions and exercises ahead, so get out your pen and journal and take the time needed to work through the following pages. Ready?

Visions begin with the decision to be truthful about what is and isn't working in your life, and the areas that you feel "stuck" in. Creating a vision for all the pieces of your life will help produce conscious living; even the areas that are working well. Take some time to write the vision that you have, so that, as life evolves, you will have a statement to measure the changes and growth. The Life Vision Wheel is a great tool for helping you evaluate your life in pieces and as a whole. Look closely at Sandra's Life Vision Wheel and then write in what makes up your life (remember yours will look different). Write 1 to 8 with 1 being by the area that functions the <u>best</u> in your life and moving to 8, the one that isn't functioning as well as you would like. We encourage you to pick two areas to start with and use them as you work through this chapter. Of course, we strongly encourage you to continue to work on all the areas of your Life Vision Wheel far after the pages of this book leave your hands. We'd like to add, from many years of doing this evaluation with ourselves and professionally with others, you should never reach a time when you say, "All the areas of my life are functioning perfectly." There is always room for growth and improvement – welcome and un-welcomed – but that is a part of being alive. Once you grasp the power of identifying areas that need work, along with the ability to brainstorm about a new vision (complete with goals and a plan that aligns with your core values and beliefs), it isn't as scary, lonely or overwhelming. You have now created a road map and compass for the next journey.

YOUR TRANSFORMATION

Creating a Life Vision Wheel: Use the life circle graphic to plot the areas of your life you most want to work on at this time. Sandra's life circle is here for you to use as an example.

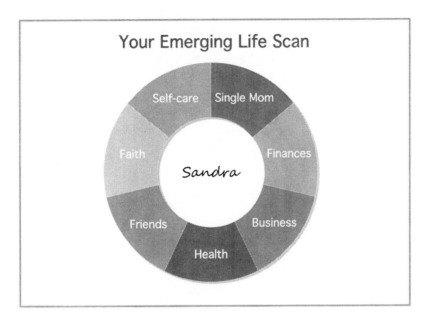

Areas I am stuck on today and need to work on:

1. Health

   a. Learning to eat more consciously

   b. Exercise regularly

2. Friendships

   a. Being more intentional about scheduling time to be with friends

   b. Nurturing my dearest friendships

3. Scheduling more downtime for myself

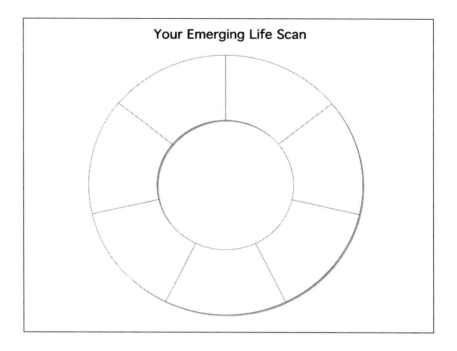

Living Life with Purpose and Meaning

The "mission" is the motivational aspect of vision: it defines and clarifies why your life vision matters, the values that govern your life and what is important to you. After divorce, women may feel a sense of loss and direction because their mission was so intertwined with their marriage; being a wife, mother, and all of the identities that were enmeshed with their married life. To be successful in your rebuilding, you have to now work on your mission, purpose and vision as a single woman and understand that some of those identities and associations will change, while others will be redefined, and some will remain the same.

YOUR TRANSFORMATION
The following questions will help you identify your mission and purpose.

1. **What am I here on this earth to do?**

2. **What kind of legacy do I want to leave?**

3. **What kind of life do I want to lead?**

4. **Does my life look like the life I desire?**

So much of what motivates and inspires us to make changes and take action lies within the "why." A mission statement is central in defining our internal motivation. It defines "why" life and change matter. By officially declaring your vision, you will have your own personal compass. This compass will offer you insightful directions when you are lost, it will alert you when you are getting off course, and it will kindly welcome you when you have arrived at your destination. Combined with your vision and goals you will become focused in everything from your daily choices and actions, to achieving your long-term goals.

There will always be a need or crisis to take you off your path. Knowing your purpose and mission is kind of like having your own lighthouse that guides you through the storms of life (parenting issues, work, self-care, relationships, spiritual walk, etc.) and will not allow you to drift out to sea.

Having this kind of clarity for your life after your divorce will be instrumental in moving forward. It also allows you to release things in your life that are toxic or robbing you of your energy (this includes the areas you identified in *Chapter 4: Invisible Prison Walls*).

Your purpose should absolutely tap into what energizes you and makes you hopeful. It should reflect your passion, your desires, and core being which all come from self awareness. Purpose should be anchored in love (God) and not fear. Purposes to be married, wealthy, accepted, etc. are fear-based. Purpose is from your soul where God has safely placed it within you. He created you, and your divorce hasn't changed His plan or your purpose one bit. Take some time to pray and journal. What energizes you? What thoughts and ideas have been with you most of your life before you covered them up with roles and rules of life? What resonates with your soul and emotions?

There are no right or wrong mission statements or life purposes. The only rule for defining one is that it must be your own. However, keep in mind, when your God-given purpose is in contradiction with the life you are living, you will always feel unsettled. Divorce often has the empowerment to bound people by their circumstances and they lose sight of their purpose or mission. This is fallacy. Divorce is a chapter in your life story; it is not you, your purpose nor should it ever define you. There may be a lot of odds stacked against you; the mountain may seem too steep some days, but remember you do matter and your life matters and you are loved! Persevere on our friends!

Your purpose is written in your soul, but your mission statement is written out of your purpose and states your objective of life. It should be short, concise and to the point. It should be written as an action. Remember, your purpose is the trigger that puts your mission into action.

YOUR TRANSFORMATION

Write your mission and purpose statements.
(Example: To love God, love myself, love my family and love others through my daily words and actions.)

Next, let's focus on your big picture vision. What we are going to ask you to do now may seem a little silly at first, but stay with us here. It can literally be life-changing. Have you spent much time brainstorming? You know, pen to paper, pie in

the sky—-throw out even your wildest ideas and options about your life. We want you to brain-storm about the life you desire.

The life I desire...
(Examples: I would like to travel around the world for one year. I would like to write a book.)

List 3 to 5 things that make you happy
(Examples: Sitting on my porch swing reading. Walking into my organized closets.)

What are 3 to 5 things you are committed to in your life?
(Example: Creating an "individual" relationship with my children.)

List 3 to 5 things you are doing right now to use your full potential
(Example: Taking some on-line courses regarding finances.)

Write down 3 to 5 of your most important roles and then write down 5 adjectives that describe your behavior in each of these roles:

List 3 to 5 things you would like to do to make a difference in this world. I can make a difference in this world by ...
(Example: Taking time to thank people, compliment people and share with others how much I appreciate and treasure them.)

Strategic Visioning:

Take time to be quiet. Spend some time alone, daydream, write down what comes to mind, leaf through magazines; tear out pictures that speak to you. They should trigger strong emotions (a peaceful woman taking a walk on the beach; a quote that inspires you; a trip you wish to take). You are doing these things to create a vision board. You can pick up a white board at Target, Wal-Mart or a local craft store. We like ones that are a little more durable (they need to stick around for awhile!), but you pick the one that works for you. Cut and paste some of the pictures that speak to the life you wish to live; write some personal messages and visions. A "vision board" is kind of like a picture of your soul being lived out – pictures say more than a thousand words.

Remember, a vision board won't create your life. It is the picture and location for which to set your compass toward; then you can design the map. Nothing will happen from there if you don't move to action by putting one foot in front of the other and begin walking into your new life: one vision, one goal, and one action at a time.

Using your answers to the questions along with your vision board and your core values, begin writing your vision statement. You now have a picture to help you create the road map to arrive at this life you have envisioned. Remember, we all continue to grow and evolve as life changes, so over time your vision will follow suit.

Sandra's Vision Board she created
right after her divorce:

Wizard of Oz pictures – these characters
(fiction as they may be) – caused me to really
follow their "yellow brick road" of seeking
what God had already placed in their hearts.
They faced their fears and stayed the course
to find their way.

Women at the beach; woman in the chair –
all showing a sense of peacefulness with
their life and they are alone.

Tug of rope game – reminder that someone
has to put down the rope to stop the war.

Charm bracelet – the circle of family and
importance of them

Boat – Sandra's passion for boating and I
wanted to reconnect with that.

Luggage – it's red and I realized that when I
went to buy luggage it didn't have to be
black. I could be bold and different.

Flowers – how much I love fresh flowers.
They rejuvenate me and remind me of hope
and growth.

City street – I dreamed of going to Maine on
vacation – and I went in 2006.

Well, here you are now looking at a board with a life you hope and pray one day is yours; if only you could close your eyes and click your red slippers together three times and land there. Oh no, that would be too easy. There is more to be done and continual need for perseverance and patience with and for yourself. Read and work on.

Strategic Planning:

This is the process that provides specific direction and meaning to the day-to-day activities for you. Strategic planning places the strategic vision into motion. It will help identify all the steps and timelines to meet the vision. It enables effective pursuit of a specific goal or result. This will include prioritizing goals along with options and obstacles to navigate. The over-arching clarity and strategies gained for your life vision will be amazing and life altering.

Goals:

Goals help you find new knowledge and abilities that let you experience growth as you build your life. The seasons leading up to divorce, and certainly the divorce process, rob us of perspective and vision. The only real goal during those times is usually surviving the day. Designing your new vision and setting new goals will help with seeing your future with clarity, depth and new perspective.

Setting goals can give structure to your life and help tame the chaos from an unstructured journey. Goals direct, energize and motivate you. Meeting your goals is extremely rewarding. Goals are essential keys in aiding you to achieving a new start.

Goals give you single focuses, whereas your vision and purpose give you a broad, directional focus to move your life forward. You will have a better understanding of where you should spend your time and energy. Goals help reel you in when you get sidetracked or swept away by the currents of everyday life.

Accountability is stronger when you have set goals; which helps you to stay true to your core values, vision, purpose and life vision. Goals also help you grow by moving you out of the "safe" places in your life and toward your vision and being the best you. Without goals you may take the path of least resistance or leave your vision on your board and not give it the feet, arms and voice to become your life. Goals help us overcome barriers to get to what's on the other side. This is powerful as you define your "new" normal.

Goal statements are written once you have a vision in place. You should have a strategic plan for each of your goals. Write your vision(s) then write your goals for each vision. Your goals should include options for reaching them along with the obstacles you should anticipate encountering. Write down who will help you reach each goal (this can include resources, education, phone calls, internet research, setting up a meeting with someone, asking for others for help). Make sure the goal is moving you closer to your vision. Be specific with your goals and always write them in a positive manner. Place a time frame on your goal and always make the goal measurable. Celebrate each success, big and small as you accomplish your goals!

Take note when setting your goals to not make the common mistake of proclaiming a goal that is actually an end result and not the actual goal. For instance, "My goal is make a lot of money." This statement is actually the end result. Organizing, planning, gaining education, managing, developing a budget are all goals set to achieve the end result. A goal is to make a difference, to make things better than they were yesterday, to make a contribution to life and society. Setting the right goals and working hard to achieve them will eventually result in success.

Another thing to keep in mind is that open-ended goals lead to life passing us by. When you have goals attached to time frames, you are accountable and will maximize your time, energy, and experiences during your God-given days here on earth. With a clear vision, you will fully understand your present reality and stretch toward your desired future. I know all women pray to hear our Lord say to us one day, "Well done my faithful servant. You lived the life I gave you with purpose and passion." God knows the trials and setbacks we experience, but He still encourages us on to the land of milk and honey. That is why we pray for all divorced women to rise out of the ashes of their divorce and emerge into their new beginning with a renewed vision for their growth and the life waiting on them.

A Personal Message from Sandra:

This chapter is not any different than the rest of this book — I only write about what I have already lived. I wish I were a wise teacher without having to live out my lessons. Clarifying my core values, writing my mission statement (for many areas of my life) and creating new visions were some of the most impactful growth tools I used in rebuilding my own life after divorce. I still use these in my personal and professional life — it works — I promise.

I would like to share a personal story about how I created a vision for me and my children and our home.

The first few days following my separation I saw emptiness all over our home. The master bedroom suit was gone, along with a sofa, table and chairs, lamps, and pictures. Everywhere we looked it was a visual reminder of how our lives had just changed dramatically. I thought it was one thing for me to see this, but for my children to see it was just too much to bear. I was the adult and knew the reason for the departure of these household goods, but for the kids, it just looked empty and they didn't understand why the items were gone.

I certainly could have slept on the couch until there was enough money to buy a bed, but I knew that my kids would feel sorry for me. What would they say or feel when friends came over and saw the house? The awkwardness was just so apparent, but there simply wasn't any money to purchase new items.

Right in the middle of my emotional tidal waves and fearful state of being (and my legal maze), I still knew that our home had to be a safe refuge to offer us some peace and stability. This became my first vision that aligned with my core value of family and created my goal to make our house look like a home again. My obstacle was that I had no money. My options were to ask for help and donations (my value drove my vision more than my pride). I put a time frame on my goal – immediately top priority – even above my emotions, and all the other demands pulling at me.

I moved furniture around and made a list of some items that would help pull the house back together. I shared with my support group of women that I didn't have bedroom furniture and explained about all the other pieces missing. Women always amaze me with their hearts and love for their sisters. One woman had a sofa in storage that she wasn't using and she and her husband brought it over. Another lady who worked at the front desk of my daughter's elementary school called one morning and said, "The strangest thing just happened, (we know it isn't strange – we call these "God moments") I received a call from someone who is redoing her guest bedroom and wanted to know if I knew of anyone that needed a queen size bed, mattress and springs." Her reply, "You are an answer to prayers." I borrowed a truck that afternoon and loaded the bed and the linens, comforter, shams, bed skirt – all of it! What a beautiful gift! As I write this, I just had tears in my eyes once again. Within a week, our home looked different, but it certainly looked like home and not like half our life was just carried out the front door.

This is just one of my many vision stories – I have done this for holidays, financials, my career, vacations and for every "new" or "next" step in my life journey. My hope for you, dear sister, is that you, too, find a vision—a purpose—and live your life to its absolute fullest. You are a child of God. Even if you cannot see the light up ahead, visualize it; live it; breathe it. And soon, your "it" will be your reality.

Sandra

A Personal Message from Jennifer:

I was blessed to work with a Christian psychiatrist who challenged me to write mission and vision statements for my life in my early 20s. That exercise and the resulting statements have been profound and powerful tools for making decisions throughout my adult life. I actually have separate mission and visions statements. Different coaches use the terms in different ways, so I would like to clarify how I use the terms and how I constructed my own statements for my life. A written definition for a mission statement as it is used in the corporate world is, "a formal, short, written statement of the purpose of a company or organization". A mission statement should do the following:

- *guide the actions of the organization (individual)*
- *spell out overall goals*
- *provide a sense of direction*
- *guide decision making*

I like this definition and say it works perfectly for me as well. Therefore, the definition of my personal mission statement is "a formal, short, written statement of the purpose of Jennifer Cisney" which will guide my actions, spell out overall goals, provide a sense of direction and guide decision making. Who couldn't use that?

Because the mission statement is so broad, you need to think broadly. My psychiatrist friend actually told me that my mission statement answered the questions "why are you here?" or "what are you good for?" I took into consideration several factors including my gifts and talents, my passions and interests and my intentions. In looking at those things over the course of my life, they all centered on communication. The key "action" in my mission statement is to communicate or communicating. Whether it is in written form, such as this book, or through media like video, radio, public speaking or via the internet, or direct conversation like in my counseling and coaching, nearly all of my professional life has involved communication. But in addition to action, your mission statement should include "values" that inform your actions. For me, it was stating a purpose for my communication. Any action can be either positive or negative. For me, some of the guiding values that inform my communication are truth and helping provide a better quality of life for others. I always want to make sure that my communication is both truthful and helpful to others. This is the key reason I left my first career path in broadcast journalism. As a TV news reporter, my actions were focused on communication, but without the values that were so important to me. I was not able to communicate in that role in ways I felt were always truthful and focused on providing help or a better quality of life for others.

The "vision" for my life, as I define it, is more about the "who" than the "what". My vision statement is about my being the person I want to become and not so much about the doing or the work of my life. I feel blessed in that I did not construct my vision statement. That came directly from God. I believe God gave me a vision for the person He wants me to become during a spiritual retreat in 1997. I can certainly say that my first reaction was "I will never be able to achieve this". But I trust God. I have certainly not reached this goal, but I am closer. Sometimes it feels as if I take one step forward and two steps back, but I always keep in mind the vision for the woman God wants me to be as my objective and focus. It would take a long time to explain this vision and it is deeply personal, but let me just say it is about becoming a woman of truth, authenticity and courage. God gave me a vision for becoming a woman who is concerned only about pleasing God and honoring Him and has no concern about pleasing others or worldly success or achievement. Like I said, I am not there yet (not even close). But each day, this vision informs my decisions and I ask myself if each action or choice will move me toward that vision or away from it.

Jennifer

My Quilt

* * *

As I faced my maker at the last judgment, I knelt before the Lord along with all the other souls. Before each of us laid our lives like the squares of a quilt in many piles.

An angel sat before each of us sewing our quilt squares together into a tapestry that is our life. But as my angel took each piece of cloth off the pile, I noticed how ragged and empty each of my squares was.

They were filled with giant holes. Each square was labeled with a part of my life that had been difficult, the challenges and temptations I was faced with my everyday life. I saw hardships that I endured, which were the largest holes of all. I glanced around me. Nobody else had such squares. Other than a tiny hole here and there, the other tapestries were filled with rich color and the bright hues of worldly fortune.

I gazed upon my own life and was disheartened. My angel was sewing the ragged pieces of cloth together, threadbare and empty, like binding air. Finally the time came when each life was to be displayed, held up to the light, the scrutiny of truth.

The others rose, each in turn, holding up their tapestries. So filled their lives had been. So filled their lives had been. My angel looked upon me, and nodded for me to rise. My gaze dropped to the ground in shame. I hadn't had all the earthly fortunes. I had love in my life, and laughter. But there had also been trials of illness, and death, and false accusations that took from me my world as I knew it. I had to start over many times. I often struggled with the temptation to quit, only to somehow muster the strength to pick up and begin again. I spent many nights on my knees in prayer, asking for help and guidance in my life. I had often been held up to ridicule, which I endured painfully, each time offering it up to the Father in hopes that I would not melt within my skin beneath the judgmental gaze of those who unfairly judged me.

And now, I had to face the truth. My life was what it was, and I had to accept it for what it was. I rose and slowly lifted the combined squares of my life to the light. An awe-filled gasp filled the air. I gazed around at the others who stared at me with wide eyes. Then, I looked upon the tapestry before me. Light flooded the many holes, creating an image, the face of Christ.

Then our Lord stood before me, with warmth and love in His eyes. He said, "Every time you gave over your life to Me, it became My life, My hardships, and My struggles. Each point of light in your life is when you stepped aside and let Me shine through, until there was more of Me than there was of you."

•   •   •

Author Unknown

***A special note from Sandra and Jennifer:
Don't we all want to spend our time on earth allowing God's light to shine through our lives? In Isaiah's prophecy, in 61:3, God wants us to display His splendor. God says we're like "precious jewels". He wants to use us to reflect His own light and beauty. God looks at us and sees a treasure, a fine jewel. Sure, there has been divorce, there has been sin, and there have been imperfections. We live in a flawed world. Through God's word, we know He has never expected us to be flawless in this life here on earth. Our created purpose is to let God's light shine through us in ways no one else can. Whoever authored this poem certainly understood God's love and His light that shines through our broken lives. Shine sisters, shine!

Chapter 8

Saying Hello to Your Future

L ife is a gift from God; how we live it is our gift to God. If we accept each day as a gift from our Father's hand, we may also hear a voice whispering an invitation to open our new beginning with Him. That is the purpose behind this book, coupled with the strength and encouragement we hope that you have gained throughout these pages. We have truly cherished this time as we walked this journey beside you, and we are proud of the important steps you have taken to make this your best life.

Our journeys have all looked different, but we are all sisters together. As the saying goes, "She has walked a mile in my shoes." Divorce is now a part of your life's fabric. We don't get to cut out bits and pieces of this life, but as we've discussed, we do get to choose how we will live forward with the squares of our quilt. There are wounds from the divorce, some have left scars, but they are no longer bleeding. You are learning to embrace the parts of your life you choose to hold onto and say good-bye to the parts that are no longer serving you, your family, your life or your Lord well.

So we ask, "Have you decided how the next chapter of your life is going to be lived?" Divorce may have taken a lot of you with it, but you have so much life left to live! Our hope and prayer is that you have started to design your own personal life road map. Our souls are here on earth to experience life in human form, and boy, have you experienced some life! Now it is time to write some life. Your life story is one of a kind, just like the butterfly: you are uniquely designed. Your transformation begins with you, freeing yourself from your cocoons (your bindings), and flying as you co-author, with God, the rest of the story.

We make choices everyday and the sum of those choices make up our life. Today, choose to **Emerge Victoriously** into your future by embracing your journey. The road will have curves, sharp turns, steep hills; these are called obstacles, but remember that negativity, fear, blame and excuses are the biggest supporters of obstacles. Your desire to value this precious time assigned to each and every life and the blood that it cost to purchase this life will be your energy to push you forward as you invest, grow and rebuild your life after divorce.

You now know more than ever that God hasn't taken you out of His bigger story for your life and we pray you won't opt out either. You are conscious of how your values, beliefs, life mission and purpose statements are the heart behind designing your vision. You have learned this will dictate the goals as you map your life path with the greatest of intention. Each day is a new opportunity to move you one step closer to the life you wish to live. We love this quote by Diane Ackerman, "I don't want to get to the end of my life and find out that I lived just the length of it. I want to have lived the width of it as well."

As you continue to sew new squares into your quilt, decide how your divorce is written in your life story. Be intentional about making some good memories. These will be the pictures of your heart, your voice, as you speak into other's lives, and the legacy you are leaving for all those you have loved and who love you. There are the squares of divorce, anger, resentment, but there are these squares that follow; they are the ones of hope, resilience, faith, and willingness to keep evolving. The memories your children and loved ones will hold in their hearts are: "She was willing to smile again, to dream again, to offer grace again and to see the good in the day and, most importantly, to see God's hand at work in her life." Isn't that what we all wish for? By doing this stage of our life well, we are opening the door for everyone to see that we are continuing to live a life of clarity and honor. You know who you are, what you believe and you no longer live in shame, guilt and confusion. You are not walking through life with the residual words and attitudes from your divorce. You are transforming with each stroke of the paint brush on the blank canvas of your next page.

As Christian women, our hope and faith rests in the never ending story of how God continues to take things the world sees as death and create new life. Spring always follows winter. Next time you see a wild flower (daisy, sunflowers, green grass, etc.) think of their first appearances and how they struggled to break through the hard ground after months of cold and ice. They seem so small and vulnerable, but they are deceptively strong. Those tiny stems push and prod their way through the soil and grow toward the light. They want to live, they want to show their beauty, and by faith, they know there is only a season for them to emerge, but they will be back. This is the theme we read through scripture, this is Easter, it is the story of the butterfly, will you allow it to be your story too?

A Personal Message from Sandra and Jennifer:

We have come to accept that we won't ever have it all together or all figured out this side of heaven. With that being said, we wake up each day choosing to be the best we can be for that day. We keep our eyes on our vision boards and the lives we believe we are here to live – not the life that someone else is here to live – but ours. We don't do everyday well, but we honestly can say we try to learn from what isn't working well and seek a better way.

Divorce has forever changed us and our lives, but it does not define us! We live with it as a passenger, but will not let it drive. We are going to share the front seat with God. We trust that He has the whole picture on His vision board. We just keep trying to live with a plan, our goals and hope that leads us closer to His vision. And when we mess up – which happens often – we do not let the negative words and judgment of others stop us. We are comfortable with our lives.

Today we know:
- *Each day happens but once and living in the past will rob us of living in this present day.*

- *There is complete lack of clarity in saying, "If I can just get through this situation, problem or change, everything will be all right." That is a temporal statement and there are always new problems, changes and situations to take the place of the last ones. Some are more intense than others and some are bigger or smaller – but they will come. But what we also know is there is complete trust in knowing that we get to choose our attitudes which will be powerful in helping us navigate through the change, problem or situation.*
- *We are sinners in need of forgiveness. We have wounded many others and we have learned the lessons of why God instructs us to forgive. He wishes for us to forgive so we can free our souls and not stay chained and bound to the ugliness and destruction of a life lived through resentment and anger. Forgiveness allows our souls to be free to live in relationship with the trinity – which is full of love.*
- *We have failed ourselves and others but we are not failures. We are valuable jewels to Him – just like you – and God loves everyone – not the sin or failures but ME and YOU.*
- *We need grace. We need to offer grace.*

- *We have a vision and a plan for ourselves and our lives, but we also know we are to be a vessel willing to allow God to alter those plans for Him and we are to be a faithful participant. He already knows when we will kick, scream and complain. He knows that fear will be a companion for this life time – but He also knows that if we choose to allow Him to walk with us the next chapter will be the one that needs to be written.*

Life requires a lot to be forgiven, mistakes to be learned from, and wounds to be healed. Degrees, money, positions, and even being a Christian will not inoculate us from living in this fallen world. What will really matter in the end is how we loved and touched others in our lives. It has taken a lot of life lessons, pain and hardships to arrive at the door of these things that we know for sure. We don't say them to sound good or like we are some spiritual expert. We say them because they are true to us and we hope by offering them to you will empower your growth and healing in some way. We have no idea who should receive the credits for the words they penned, but we want to leave you with this prayer:

May the light of God surround me.
May the love of God enfold me.
May the power of God protect me.
May the presence of God watch over me,
and may I never forget wherever I am, God is.

*As we said earlier in the book, we may have never met (and we are still hoping we get the chance). We pray for you and for the growth and healing you so deserve. We also pray for the courage to say you wish to live a bigger life than a divorced life. **Emerge Victoriously**, our sister, as you design your life by choosing to transform.*

Love and Blessings on your journey as you write the next chapter of your life story.

Fly beautifully with grace, peace and love,

Sandra & Jennifer

Endnotes

Bridges, Jeff. <u>Pursuit of Holiness</u>. (Colorado Springs, Co: Nav Press Publishing, 1996).

Lewis, C.S. <u>The Four Loves</u>. (Ft. Washington, PA: Harvest Books, 1960).

Hart, Archibald D. <u>The Anxiety Cure</u>. (Nashville, TN: Thomas Nelson, 1999).

Seamands, David. <u>Healing for Damaged Emotions</u>. (Colorado Springs, CO: Chariott Victor Publishing, 1991).

Shain, Merle. <u>When Lovers Are Friends</u>. (New York, NY: Bantam Books, 1978).

Beattie, Melody. <u>The Language of Letting Go</u>. (Center City, MN: Hazelden Publishing, 1990).

Townsend, John and Cloud, Henry. <u>Boundaries</u>. (Grand Rapids, MI: Zondervan Corp, 2002).

• • •

Additional Products and Resources

• • •

Check out our other **Emerge Victorious** Products:

"Emerge Victorious, the Next Step in Rebuilding Your Life After Divorce"** is an interactive DVD video series with the purpose of helping women grow through and beyond their divorce. This series features Christian professionals in their field of expertise offering practical tools, guidance and encouragement. The videos and accompanying companion workbook will help women transform their lives. The videos may be purchased individually, or in sets to use with a group. These are also great resources and tools for coaches and counselors to use in their practice.

Topics addressed:
- Forgiveness
- Dating
- Sexuality
- Spirituality
- Career
- Finances
- Single parenting / Co-parenting
- Self-care and Women's Health
- Building Relationships
- Moving On
- 50+ and rebuilding life after divorce
- Divorce without children

"Emerge Victorious, A Woman's Transformational Journal" is an excellent companion to **Emerge Victorious, A Woman's Transformational Guide After Her Divorce**, or as your separate journal to help you with clarity, purpose and vision as you step into the next chapter of your life.

Please visit us at:
www. EmergeVictorious.com
800-615-6708
info@EmergeVictorious.com

Other books you may want to read:
Lord, I just want to Be Happy by Leslie Vernick (Harvest House)

<u>Taking Out Your Emotional Trash</u> by Georgia Shaffer (Harvest House)

<u>How Not To Date a Looser</u> by Georgia Shaffer (Tyndale House)

<u>The Five Love Languages of Apology</u> by Gary Chapman and Dr. Jennifer Thomas (Northfield Publishing)

<u>The Fresh Start, Divorce Recovery Workbook</u> by Bob Burns and Tom Whiteman (Thomas Nelson Publishers)

<u>The Courage to Be a Single Mother</u> by Sheila Ellison (Harper Collins Publishers)

CPSIA information can be obtained at www.ICGtesting.com
Printed in the USA
BVOW010956190911

271465BV00002B/4/P